E Special,
31

Krozk

THE AMAZING WORLD OF KRESKIN

Random House  New York

THE AMAZING WORLD OF KRESKIN

BY KRESKIN

Library of Congress Cataloging in Publication Data

Kreskin, 1935–
  The amazing world of Kreskin.

  1. Kreskin, 1935–   2. Psychical research.
3. Occult sciences. I. Title.
BF1027.K75A3   133.8′092′4 [B]   72–11411
ISBN 0–394–48440–1

First Edition

To
Mom and Dad, and Marien
to whom, twenty years ago,
I promised I'd dedicate my
first book

AUTHOR'S NOTE

As a performer, a "mentalist," for lack of a better self-description, I spend several hours daily in concert halls, before college audiences, or in front of TV cameras, exploring the scientific field of parapsychology.

To amuse, intrigue, cause wonder, I "suggest" to people that they have been transported to the Arctic. Suddenly they shiver, without the nonsense of a "hypnotic trance." I tell them that they are moon people and they begin to converse in "moon talk," drawing on an incredible pool of hidden imagination. Nonverbally, I direct them to a single name in a phone book. Out of thousands, they select it correctly. Through a kind of telepathy, I am often successful at thought perception.

I do not claim to know the "how" and "why" of these responses. But apparently I'm in rather truthful company because most reputable parapsychologists admit that beyond theory they do not have the slightest idea of the true nature of extrasensory perception. Nor can they explain the unstable psychic phenomena termed *psi* which supposedly keys ESP.

While I'm always in awe of the mental tools with which I

work, I'm not in awe of the field itself. Why should we be reverent or mystical about something that is a part of everyone? From that standpoint, the phenomena begs for exploration. Further, all of us are living laboratories of the mind, so research cannot be limited to a handful of psychologists and psychiatrists.

Unlike medical or university laboratory test subjects undergoing experimentation in sharply defined areas, my ESP volunteers are audiences of several hundreds up to thousands —all "off the streets." They react normally and spontaneously without the more or less controlled conditions of experimental parapsychology. I think it is a plus.

Yet I have learned and relearned one constant: *We know so very little of the workings and true capabilities of the human mind.* No week, month or year has gone by that I haven't been baffled by the responses, challenged by the unknown.

For years, as both a stage and occasional clinical "hypnotist," I was under the grand delusion that I was putting people to sleep, elaborately entrancing them according to a formula that dates back to Dr. Franz Anton Mesmer. Actually, I think I was "hypnotizing" myself. Then I discovered I could do exactly the same thing with the subject wide awake by use of a developed form of *suggestibility.*

As of now, I do not think that "hypnosis," with its sleeplike trance, exists. It is somewhat a well-meant fraud. I don't believe that the "sleep trance" has ever existed except as a cooperative and acted imaginative response from the subject. Cleverly guided into a role, Sleeping Beauty is very much awake, peering mentally with shrewd eyes.

In the pages that follow, covering my experiences in entertainment ESP as well as "hypnosis," with a few negative reactions to mediums, seers and the like, I would prefer to offer an exact scientific explanation of what occurs when I perceive a thought or suggest a sky full of flying saucers. Unfortunately, I can only reveal how I attempt to do it, and how it works for me.

We may not know the answers for another century. Perhaps we'll never really know, but we should try to find out. Hopefully, ESP will one day be reversed to mean *phenomena scientifically explained.*

Many hours of taped memories, hundreds of questions went into this book. Probing constantly was writer Theodore Taylor, who took on the task of organizing the material and placing it into manuscript form. On show business hours, we worked in dressing rooms and hotels in Las Vegas and California before and after performances. I remember one midnight taping session in a waiting room at Los Angeles International Airport. Nearby a suspected hijacker was being frisked by security guards. It seemed so strange to be talking about poltergeists and mediums at that moment.

KRESKIN
Easton, Pa.
March 1973

CONTENTS

PART I
ESP AS
ENTERTAINMENT

[1]

The unknown is always there. Where do you stop?

Not long ago, during a concert before students and faculty at Rutgers University, a young lady stood up in the front row after I'd revealed a thought. She'd been concentrating on a single subject and I'd received it.

"Someone here is thinking of her boyfriend," I remember saying.

She was a pretty blonde, about nineteen or twenty.

Moving closer to her, I said, "Think of his name, please. Concentrate on it very hard." This is the usual phraseology for thought-perception demonstrations, as simple and direct as I can make it.

Facial muscles and eyes soon indicated that she was concentrating deeply. In a moment I gave her the name.

"Think of his address, please," I then said.

She concentrated a moment longer and I perceived that thought, naming the correct street, street number and town.

The audience, thankfully, was hushed, making it easier for us to communicate. Quiet sharpens the signals.

"His phone number," I requested.

The pretty blonde again concentrated and I was able to call out the digits.

By this time I realized that she was a near-perfect subject and could not resist probing on. "Do you have any brothers or sisters?" I asked.

She nodded.

"Think of their names, please."

This took a bit longer but I finally named each one—two brothers and two sisters. The names came in distinctly. I received them almost visually—a common occurrence.

"Now their birth dates, please. Think of their birth dates by name. If you can't remember the exact date, the month will be okay."

Again, she concentrated and I picked up the information, spieling it off.

Suddenly I was aware that the young lady was becoming hysterical. We'd now been in this half verbal, half mental communication for six or seven minutes, more time than I'd ever devoted to a single thought-perception routine in any public concert.

Oddly enough, I found myself beginning to shake too. I'd opened up her mind as well as my own. We were mentally locked onto each other. I stopped immediately. Yet, without this nervous reaction from the uneasiness of crossing into a current twilight territory, a definitely mutual reaction, I'm certain we could have gone on for two hours. However, I vowed then and there to limit, for the time being, such adventuring to a few single thoughts. No person is prepared for an extended mental exchange when it does happen. It is eerie only because it is not customary.

4

Thinking about it later, I realized that the communication had almost approached the mechanical. Standing about eight feet away from her, I had hardly been aware of her physical presence. The information was received but not evaluated, then relayed to the audience. They, too, at least for me, ceased to exist. As the minutes went by, the tuning became finer; each thought was clear and distinct. For seven minutes we were invisibly and strangely linked.

I am not a "psychic."

I'm not a *mind reader*, because that implies I could totally penetrate the processes of the human brain and receive chains of thoughts. On many occasions I can perceive a single thought or a series of single, simple thoughts if the subject is properly tuned to me. I think this silent communication is within the capability of many people, once trained and self-sensitized.

Above all, I'm not a "medium."

I do not give *readings* of any type. I cannot converse with spirits. I don't and can't predict the future, and I am not sure that anyone can. I fly by commercial jet and not by *astral projection*. I do not subscribe to the occult. Decidedly, I have enough trouble living in this universe without putting an intruding foot into another ghostly world. Regretfully, I'm not gifted with any supernatural power.

Perhaps some of what I do fits into the category of "psychic," so-called, under certain conditions. But I think that my particular forms of mental communication, as adapted for the stage, are probably hypersensitive or hypernormal rather than extrasensitive. In the manner of a concert pianist who has spent much of his life at the keyboard, the communication, a very earthly one so far as I'm concerned, has been developed through years of painstaking practice.

Using only imagination I can "see" a white rabbit on that table over there. Now he moves, turns, looks. This is not psychic. It is within the capability of almost anyone who is willing to sharpen and sensitize imagination.

For my purpose the brain, container for the mind, is

considerably more receptive to training than a leg muscle. If the leg muscles can be coordinated to run a hundred-yard dash in less than ten seconds, it is reasonable to expect that the most perfected human machinery of all can be trained to go far beyond the commonly accepted senses.

A great deal that occurs in parapsychology is no doubt related to senses in terms we've never been able to compartmentalize. They've been blurred into the term extrasensory perception, popularized by the renowned pioneer Dr. Joseph B. Rhine, formerly of Duke University. But ESP is an abortive contradiction, suggesting we have the ability to perceive beyond our senses. Really, how is that possible? Perhaps we should just expand our range of senses, blindly, to seven or eight? Who's to know that eighteen or twenty-two don't exist?

A previous pioneer, Dr. Sigmund Freud, once theorized that our psychic abilities were diminishing. All of our senses have suffered because of the technical revolution. Assaulted by machinery, traffic, aircraft and screaming rock guitars, we are losing fine-hearing. It follows that if we all became mute tomorrow it is quite possible we'd develop another sense. Survival might force the oddity of telepathy into the normal and everyday. The "sense," certainly, is already there. It isn't paranormal.

True, I've produced manifestations, or effects, that might be attached to the somewhat questionable "psychic senses" area, and again I confess I don't understand many of them. Obviously something happens to me and suddenly I'm talking about things that I should not, in the conscious awareness, know. At the same time, I don't believe this is "psychic," as we commonly accept the word. Likely, the awareness is triggered because of the aforementioned trained sensitivity.

Much the same thing occurs in almost every normal person. Random thoughts come to mind "out of the blue." Words are spoken not related to the immediate surrounding or events or other persons present. The unconscious, without direction, has been developing thoughts and they surface. It happens to everyone.

But beyond these common occurrences, I do pick up information through a kind of telepathy. By deep concentration, "tuning in," I seek out and then "receive" a single thought, provided the "sender" is concentrating to an almost equal depth. Some debunkers have claimed it is an ability to "muscle read" a subject's face, to decipher clues given unconsciously by the subject. This may well be a factor of ESP, as natural as an eye blink, but I am not aware of it. The reaction on the subject's face may unconsciously increase my perception of the thought, but it does not reveal the thought unless an absolute "yes" or "no" answer is involved. Anyone can usually read a positive or negative simply by studying eye register.

More than all this, if I perceive a social security number secreted in a purse at two hundred feet in a darkened theater, muscle reaction is of little help in determining the numbers and their sequence. The only source is the subject's concentration. His or her face, at that distance, is but a small shadowy object.

What I do in my concerts, as I prefer to call them, is create an extremely sensitive rapport with my audience, consciously and unconsciously. Ideally, my subjects are as much in tune with me as I am with them. They are capable of sending information by telepathy or receiving it by a combination of reverse telepathy and *suggestibility*, which is exactly what it implies.

So far as I can understand it, the mental equipment in my presentations is something outside of me, as well as within. I do not mean that I "detach" my mind. In suggestibility, I attempt to project it as strongly as possible—use it as a lever, a force. It is, in truth, spotlighted, beaming invisibly. Yet success in this communication is completely dependent on the moods and personalities of the subjects, their willingness to open their imaginations and "receive." I am helpless if they refuse.

When I walk out onstage, it is unlikely that I will be captured by any particular thought. Some nights, though, I am arrested by something that someone, usually self-primed, is trying to communicate. I no more than reach stage center when an almost electric demand is in the air. Fortunately, it doesn't happen too often. I'd rather develop the thought-perception phase through normal audience conditioning—the blend of basic theater, showmanship and psychology. However, my equipment is not the machinery of a tuned piano, nor can it be manipulated like a magical prop. And I can never absolutely predict how my subjects will respond.

In using ESP as a form of communication, I receive information in images rather than in symbols or distinct sounds. As an aid, I also practice *automatic writing* and have practiced it since childhood. It is difficult to describe precisely, but my hand writes semiconsciously or often without guided conscious thought. The hand is a direct extension of a portion of the mind which is receiving and then sending signals; another portion may be dealing with another subject, usually related. A common, less refined variation of this is the businessman who is listening on the phone, dealing with one subject while his hand is scribbling on the pad about something else.

So while talking to an audience, I'm constantly writing, although I'm not really aware of the pencil movement. The material is usually ahead of what I'm trying to say to the audience or receive from them.

As the automatic writing proceeds, and certain thoughts begin to come in clearly, a subject is developed and targeted. I then attempt to perceive through imagery. I almost see a picture, *the thought*, though not clearly; I hear information, which I don't really hear, in an auditory sense. The latter is sometimes called *clairaudience*, stealing from clairvoyance, except that I think it is just my own way of handling the information hypersensitively.

With eyes wide open I perceive the images as I'm looking out over the audience. In the case of reading someone's social security number, which seems to be a favorite because of simplicity and familiarity, I see it more easily over a darkened part of the theater. This area, far from the footlights, becomes a blackboard. The subject is dim, scarcely more than a voice.

I prefer to have the subjects in a darkened area, although it makes little difference. The lenses of my glasses resemble pop bottle bottoms. I'm helpless without them. Usually, much in the manner of a lecturing professor, I remove them entirely when perceiving thoughts. Holding them, however, does seem to aid in concentration. I have a theory that near-sightedness aids in ESP.

But the glasses are not transistorized bugging devices. I have no second set of hidden eyes, no mirror built into my ring, no periscope in my belt buckle, no assistant concealed in the ceiling and transmitting to me through a miniature radio—all of which have been advanced as "how-to" techniques.

After a Johnny Carson *Tonight* show, one critic, quite seriously, said he suspected I planted tiny mikes in numerous audience seats and then listened backstage to pick up key information as the audience chatted pre-show. What strikes me so funny about this is the picture of myself crawling around the floor at Studio B in Burbank prior to show time, stringing wires and cutting holes in upholstery. Such an NBC "Watergate" would be more hilarious than the show itself, and Carson would be better off photographing that rigging than what I do later.

On a more fundamental basis, I don't have the talents to see through the cloth of a lady's purse or through the leather of a man's wallet, wherein usually lies the small card on which the social security number is imprinted. So the only possible method is to read it with and through the mind of the cooperating sitting or standing subject. On receiving his or her signal, I project the numbers, visualizing them almost instantly. "The number is 225-12-6018."

I do not always look at what the pencil has written on my

note pad. *225-12-6018.* I am not always confident it will be correct. Most of the time, though, the written number will match the verbal projection.

From personal curiosity alone, I've sought answers to these abilities. It is annoying not to know exactly how it all works. Among others, one psychologist, Dr. Harold Hansen, advised, "Perhaps it's better that you don't know everything that's happening. It's probable that at times you're harnessing something more than you'd be able to harness if you were conscious of the mechanics." Hardly a satisfying answer for either layman or expert, yet most answers in parapsychology are seldom satisfying.

But Dr. Rhine established this hazard long ago in experiments with ESP cards at Duke. Mechanics did interfere with perception tests involving his famous cards, marked with five different symbols. First used in the early thirties, the cards are still the prime extrasensory test vehicles.

In a practical way, if I stop to analyze myself during a performance and ask myself, "Now, how the devil is this done?," I'll abruptly lose the subject's thoughts. It is only after the performance, well after, that I can afford to ponder the processes that might have taken place. Even so, I find it hard to describe them satisfactorily.

Reading this, you have a thought in mind. It is neither colored green or blue, nor triangular or round or square in shape, size or form. In physical feeling, it is probably no different from the thoughts you had twenty minutes ago. It is simply a thought, and in terms of physical reaction, not distinguishable from any other thought. An emotional thought, one of wild anger or one of deep love, does appear to have a different texture and, I suppose, "feeling." But attempt to describe that exact texture or shape or form as a separate entity! It's rather difficult.

The best I can do in answering questions is to say that the *perceived thought,* traveling invisibly, arrives in the same form as any other thought. *I accept the perceived thought; it is suddenly there, and I act upon it, without any particular evaluation.* In view of the fact that we are all using the same basic equipment, the thought, whether it is prompted by verbal or sensual contact or perceived, would cause some surprise if it arrived in a different package.

However, I firmly believe that public demonstrations of thought perception should not be considered as absolute proof of the scientific possibilities of ESP. Demonstrations such as mine should be considered as examples of the particular skills of the performer.

My own mood counts. I take a walk at least a mile long before every TV show or concert to shut out distracting thoughts around me; to build up deep introspection. I also attempt to bring myself to the point where I can discard any negative factors regarding the performance; rule out any chances of failure. Basically, I apply what Dr. Norman Vincent Peale described as the "power of positive thinking," which may well be mankind's ultimate mental tool.

[2]

During the 1890's—the early period of the British Society for Psychical Research, forerunner of the present American group —a word used to explain certain thought perceptions was *hyperaesthesia*, whereby an individual became sensitive to the slightest details in physical surroundings, the slightest changes in smell or other sensory functions. However, long before the word was formalized, the *mesmerists*, the first Svengalis, had been testing for sensitivity. They would give a subject a handkerchief, and if he was sufficiently sensitized he could find the owner by sniffing the person's hand, comparing it with the aroma of the fabric.

Another very old mesmeric experiment was to give a blank card to a subject and tell him that a picture of a loved one was on the card. The other side of the card would be marked so that it could be located after shuffling. The cards were then placed in front of the subject and his job was to select the card on which the "picture" had appeared, although it was only in his mind. Yet the subject was very often able to select that one specific blank card. His sensitivity had enabled him to pick out some special minute characteristic of the card, perhaps a flaw, and make the identification. The "picture" of the loved one which wasn't there had nothing to do with the "hit."

Some people have a natural capacity to pick out the tiniest details of any object, animate or inanimate. Others develop this capability as a skill, taking it to very sophisticated levels. A card sharp is one such "sensitive." He certainly does not buy decks of marked cards. There are only about fourteen American printed and marked "back" designs, and the professionals know the imprints of each maker. The sharp takes an ordinary deck and makes his own marks as he goes along. By the third hand, through pressures of his fingernail or hidden devices, he makes indentations, visually perceptible only to him. It is a developed sensitivity, catastrophic to the opponents in any poker game.

For entirely different purposes, solely for "tuning" and perception, I utilize all of these examples of old-fashioned hyperaesthesia. Each sense is sharpened to the highest possible degree. During a performance I am usually so highly sensitized that I can hear a needle drop in the theater or night club. I wasn't really aware of it until some years ago in the Embers Club in Indianapolis, when I suddenly blurted, "What was that?" I thought I'd heard an object fall. Perhaps a glass.

After the show was over, Bob Kaytes, the Embers' maître d', came up to say, "What you heard wasn't in the club. A waitress in the cocktail lounge dropped a tray and a glass broke." The cocktail lounge was behind a partition and the noise could not easily have penetrated into the club itself. For one thing, both rooms were soundproofed.

I began to wonder if I'd actually heard the glass break or if I had got a paranormal impression and thought I heard the noise. At any rate, I couldn't see the lounge from the stage, so it wasn't visual. For the next week I had Bob, or some other member of the staff, drop a tiny object within the club. Finally, it decreased to a needle. Now realizing for the first time that I'd sensitized my hearing to this range, it was easy to pick out the tiny click within the normal sounds of breathing, chair scraping, murmurings, ice-cube clinkings and ashtray noises. Since then I've increased the range to the point that I can usually hear a needle drop on a hard surface in a 3,000-seat auditorium, and I can often pinpoint the location. However, I must be aware that it will drop within a certain time period and alert myself to listen for it.

Certain types of sound, though, can be disastrous, especially if they're steady. Recently a gentleman at the Las Vegas Hilton kept clicking two chips in his pocket. From the stage, to my ears, they sounded like cymbals crashing. I finally stopped the performance and asked him to put the chips to better use at the craps table.

Operating under this degree of sensitivity, I usually feel exhausted, totally drained, after a concert. It takes a short while to recover. And I find it necessary to eat five meals a day simply to resupply energy. From roughly 155 of them, I usually lose two or three precious pounds per performance. Of course, complete mental concentration in a compacted time burns more energy than normal physical exertion in triple the same time.

I'm certainly not advocating ESP for weight control. Directing the stomach to push away from the table is simpler. Besides, ESP cannot be employed to cure anything, so far as is known.

[3]

I've often been asked why I use illusion, completely unrelated to parapsychology, to begin mentalism concerts. I perform card effects (I prefer "effect" to "trick" because of the mental effort involved) or join wedding rings from the audience into an unbreakable chain or insert a fifty-cent piece into a soda bottle. The latter effect, which I find great fun, is something I devised fifteen years ago. After requesting someone in the audience to lend me a quarter or a half dollar, I ask him to mark the coin for later identification. Then, bringing him up to the stage, I have him hold a soda bottle parallel to the floor, facing the audience, with one hand on the neck and the other near the base of the bottle. I then take the coin, cupped in the palm of my hand, and slam it into the base of the bottle. The audience can hear it enter and see it enter. It rolls around inside. After carrying the bottle out into the audience as evidence that the effect has worked, my volunteer returns to the stage and we smash the bottle to extract the coin. I've never been able to get it out any other way.

Admittedly, this is an act of the magi, not a mentalist. But, for one thing, I love the world of magic. I began as a child magician and will play and work at conjuring until I die. Cards are as much a part of my life as shoes. Just to keep the fingers nimble, I still work three or four hours daily with them, on jets or in hotel rooms. I enjoy the challenge of defying the eye, and mainly for my own satisfaction, am constantly trying to devise new effects. I've studied Houdini, Thurston and Blackstone endlessly to understand how they accomplished certain illusions, and this trio was never particularly concerned with any ESP manifestation. Houdini loathed psychics and mediums.

The real importance of the magic "intro" lies in the conditioning of the audience for what is to come. It took hundreds of performances to find the right combinations of conditioners prior to entering the suggestibility or ESP phases of the concerts. The ESP factor alone needs a good mental foundation to be successful.

Rapport with the audience is built up through verbal contact, and to a lesser extent, body movement. The latter is not studied but does coordinate with patter to command attention. I attempt to keep all eyes on me. I then go about creating a climate for suggestible responses, literally playing it by ear and "feel" until I can sense that the audience is ready for communication and response. The main task is to instill faith, establish a "faith-prestige" relationship early. It may take fifteen or twenty minutes but the audience is seldom aware that the program is rapidly changing from establishment of rapport and the conditioning of conjuring to an area far removed from magic. When volunteers come up onstage, they are unknowingly ready for response.

As much as possible, particularly in concerts, I attempt to involve the audience. The participation is a substantial part of the "faith-prestige" relationship; it is also plain unadulterated good showmanship.

I might say, "Do you know that you can turn a person into a lie detector? Really! We'll do it tonight and then you can try it the next time you have a party. It's a great party game. So I need twelve volunteers."

We're off and running.

I give each of the twelve persons a card, and then instruct them to select one subject to play the "guilty" person. Backstage that person will take ownership of a pocket-sized object. He will also write "*Guilty*" on a card; the other eleven subjects will write "*Innocent*" on theirs. It is impossible for the "guilty" person not to give himself away, and the majority of the audience will be able to read him.

Indeed, this is part of the standard police polygraph test. That insidious but helpful machine is a throwback to the old witch doctor who could actually read guilt. In itself it is a fearsome thing, often causing suspects to reveal themselves before being hooked to it. With its unfeeling electronic sensors, it preys on the human mind; unsympathetic, unforgiving, it is scornful, for the most part, of the mere actor, the liar.

While the subjects are backstage with their game plans, I instruct the audience to "read" the faces of each subject

15

carefully, to study the body for signs of rigidity, to attempt to catch the slightest holding of breath or blink of eye.

My players then return to the stage and I tell them to answer a flat "no" to any question I might ask, no matter what it is. I instruct them to act normally in every way, not to tip themselves with the slightest gesture. They are holding the cards face turned toward their chests.

I usually start from the left and ask each one, "Are you guilty?"

"No."

"Do you have the item?"

"No."

"Are you trying to hide your guilt from me?"

"No."

Sooner or later the person who has the object will answer the three negatives, but even the audience will be able to read the rigidity, the stress. He will reveal himself, usually by overreacting, fighting so hard not to be pinned down. The other eleven stand out in their posture of innocence.

I say, "Please turn your card."

"*Guilty*" is inscribed upon it, as well as on the face and body.

Actually, two things have occurred by now. The audience has been entertained in an interesting way; they have also, by participation, been subtly conditioned for further explorations in games concerning the mind.

As with any human interaction, no performance is the same because no audience is the same, no mood or night the same. Rainy nights are always good, for reasons beyond my comprehension. One guess is that there is a "locked-in" feeling. Oddly enough, television is an excellent platform for ESP experiences. The lights, cameras, the confined areas of the stage and audience, the closed doors—all tend to provide a fenced-in atmosphere.

The magic phase of my program comprises perhaps five to ten percent, always at the beginning, while clear-cut suggestibility is around fifty percent, with ESP, mainly thought perception, as the remainder. If I'm having difficulty establishing rapport, the ESP portion, always a challenge, might drop to fifteen percent. If we're in tune, with comparatively free communication, as there was with the girl at Rutgers, it can climb to sixty percent.

Interestingly enough, when I first experimented with ESP— though I didn't know it by that name—in my childhood magic shows, I sometimes found I could get a response by saying, "Think of something." More often than not I drew a blank and would laugh it off, whip out a deck of cards, materialize a bouquet of flowers or go into the "hypnotic" phase of the program. So I was able to find my way as an entertainer, and as the years went by I learned that I had to condition myself, as well as the audience.

As a simple example of the suggestibility phase, one of my favorites is to have someone from the audience pick a telephone book at random from a large pile of directories, open it to a specific page and put his finger on a specific name. It is then my role to announce that name. However, it is a name that I have already selected by checking the phone books. I have it in my pocket, written out before the volunteer ever walks onstage.

How is this done? How is the subject mentally commanded to target that specific name out of hundreds of thousands? Throughout the roughly two minutes, I acknowledge that I have some control of the subject's mind as each step is accomplished. I am sending positive, unmistakable mental signals. To explain as best I can, I create an intensive communication with the subject, causing him to respond involuntarily to my *sent* thought, ordering him to the correct directory, the correct page. It is a type of telepathy in reverse. The last sequence is realized by asking the subject to rotate his hand around the phone-book page, tightening the circle with each rotation. This isn't really necessary but adds to drama and audience suspense. While the subject is doing this, I stand with my back to him, mentally visualizing the circle and where his hand will stop, or should stop. If successful, it will be at the name selected prior to show time. The subject circles it firmly with a pencil.

Some ten feet away, unable to see the directory, the subject or the tiny circle that he has made, I call out *his selection*. And then wait for the affirmation and the welcome sound of applause.

Of course, he didn't select it at all. He was directed, guided, commanded, suggested into the one specific line of type. He is never aware that this nonverbal control has been exercised. Luckily, there has been about ninety-eight percent success with this particular experiment.

A more difficult version of this is done with a watch. Standing back to back, and at a distance from the subject, I instruct him to spin the hands of his watch to a specific time. Simultaneously I spin my watch hands and we will both, if successful, arrive at the same reading on the watch. In this effect, I am synchronizing to where I have *directed* him to stop. Due to rapidity of movement and the size of watch hands, success here drops to around fifty percent.

However, both experiments indicate the requirements for intense rapport and nonverbal communication. Neither effect can be accomplished without it.

The means of communication often overlap, or often combine. When I have two members of the audience come up onstage to burn four out of five small paper bags, one of which contains a hundred-dollar bill, I use both thought projection and suggestibility. I direct them *not* to select the bag containing the money. While telling them verbally to choose two bags each and strike a match to them, I am ordering them mentally to *please* by-pass the money bag. I make the nonverbal direction exceedingly clear, since it is my own hundred-dollar bill that is in danger of being crisped.

When I send four members of the audience to a supermarket with instructions to purchase four items each and place them together in a large box, I do not suggest what they should buy, verbally or mentally. However, on their return, as they concentrate deeply on the items each purchased, I use straight thought perception to identify who purchased what.

A variation of this is to retain the items in bags and then make the identification as to what has been purchased. Recently a woman mentally described her purchase as "large on one end, small on the other, and white in color." It had to be an ice cream cone, I thought. She pulled out a turnip. During the same show, another woman kept mentally describing her bagged item and I finally drew a straight line with a circle on each end on the blackboard. I was puzzled by what I was receiving from her, but relieved when she extracted a "Q-Tip." I'd also written it down.

[4]

Unlike psychometrist Peter Hurkos, I took no falls from a ladder, nor was I ever dropped on my head. Neither has any member of my family, as far back as we can trace, ever been professionally involved in magic, "hypnosis," thought perception or any psychic field. My Aunt Anna Piukutowski leaned toward it, certainly, but only as a hobby. As far as we know, no one in the Polish-Italian-American family of Kresge ever concerned himself with ESP.

I was born George, Jr., in Montclair, New Jersey, on January 12, 1935, which makes me a Capricorn, for what it is worth. My father is retired, formerly employed as a buffer by a battery company, and my mother, Lucy, is a housewife. My younger brother, Joe, is tall like my father; quiet and steady, also like my father; and he is a police officer in Caldwell, New Jersey, my hometown. It was, and is, a close and happy family. I still spend much of my available time with them.

From my mother I inherited a brisk walk and quick movements. I wish that I had truly inherited her laugh. It cuts gloom. As a kid, sitting way down front in the local movie, I'd always know when she'd joined the audience. Her laugh would be unmistakably first and last. She seldom missed a comedy. But the laughter would turn to silence whenever I began experimenting with magic. Deeply religious, she had a misunderstanding and a fear of the mystical field. She never really approved of what I was doing in the early days.

I vaguely remember the incident that sent me into show business at about the age of five. My father took me along on a visit to friends and relatives in his hometown of Bethlehem, Pennsylvania. Neither of us can recall the exact house or the name of the people, but sometime during the stay I was handed a comic book, probably to keep me occupied. A teen-ager, I think, gave me the new book which contained five or six pages of *Mandrake the Magician*. Vividly colored, electricity sparking from his fingertips and eyes, gesturing hypnotically, casting spells, crackling with excitement, Mandrake held my attention that day and for many days afterward. I came away with the book, looking at it again and again on the train home. My father does remember that much.

Over the next years I began collecting every *Mandrake* comic I could find, spending all my allowance at the newsstand. Added, soon, were *Action Comics* and *Marvel Comics*. In the back of *Marvel* was Zatara, a magician who was somewhat similar to Mandrake, using mystical powers to solve crimes. While Mandrake gestured hypnotically, Zatara would change an opponent's gun into a flower. When he wanted something to happen, he'd say it backwards. "Ogpu" meant "go up." Then he'd fly through the air. There was also Ibis the Invincible, an Egyptian who had died six thousand years ago. Reincarnated, he used a magic wand called "the Ibis stick." I lost myself in Mandrake and Zatara and Ibis. And, of course, I carved my own "Ibis stick."

Soon I began working with decks of cards and sleight of hand. While other kids were struggling on roller skates in front of our apartment house, which was located on the main street of Caldwell, I was learning the quick shuffle, trying to fan cards, manipulating them, popping them out of a sleeve. After seeing movie routines, I also learned how to juggle.

Then came "Huckle Buckle Beanstalk." To those who don't recognize it by that knee-pants name, it's the ancient game of "Hot 'n' Cold." A player leaves the room and the rest of the class hides a bean bag. The player returns and begins to look for the bag, with the class shouting "Getting hotter" or "Getting colder." I was then in the fourth grade. Wouldn't it be great, I told my parents, if the object could be found without all the directions, just by having the "hiders" think about where it was? With the blessing of childhood, I didn't know the rules—what could be done, what couldn't. I tried it with my parents and had no success, naturally. They lost interest.

But then I persuaded Joe to try it. I literally forced him to practice with me for about four months. By the end of that time I could find almost any object in our small, cluttered room without him saying "hot" or "cold." I had no idea what I was doing, nor how much I was reading his facial expressions (a lot, probably) as I neared the object, but now I realize I was blindly beginning to train myself in sensitivity and ESP.

The same year, I recall, I was given permission to study the entire psychology section, adult books, in the Caldwell public library. Not understanding one fiftieth of what I was reading, I stuck with them, eagerly awaiting the next book. All the while I remained faithful to Mandrake and kept collecting him, sometimes dreamt of him. By then I'd also heard of Houdini and the Great Thurston. Next to Mandrake, created by Lee Falk, they were my childhood heroes. Christmas of that year my parents gave me a book on Thurston.

It was quite a year. I'd learned how to pull a table cloth from beneath a set of dishes without breaking them, a juggler routine, and had demonstrated the trick in class and at assembly. About a week later Mr. Johnson, the principal, called me into the office to request that I never repeat it, much less give instructions. Dishes were being broken all over Caldwell.

But it wasn't long before I was doing a half-hour private show every Friday night at my grandparents', the Cantellos, who lived about a quarter of a mile away. My Aunt Ruth Cantello, my mother's sister, would wait at the kitchen table for me, and then summon my grandparents for the performance. I tried to display a new effect each week. They'd applaud and I'd bow.

Caldwell was then a rather rural community, trolley line to Newark running down the center of Bloomfield Avenue, flanked by huge old leafy trees. Spring and summer were delightful. With the quality of a quiet, small American town, there was plenty of running room, and fields in which to play cowboys and cops-and-robbers.

We were centrally located, to say the least. The Catholic church, where I never missed a Sunday mass, was directly across the street from our apartment. Behind us was the police station; to the left was the public library; on the other side, the only newspaper in town. On one corner was a Shell gas station, still there, now run by a close friend of mine. Bells tolled, the trolley ran; everyone knew everyone else. Christmas, Easter, the Fourth of July and Thanksgiving were sensational.

Life, as I recall it now, was mostly warm and loving, and I really didn't know the difference between "middle class" and any other class. Sunday was reserved for dinner at Grandmother Cantello's, with spaghetti the main course. I spent a lot of time in that old house, often eating weekday meals there. I listened to Aunt Ruth play the piano and eventually learned by ear, then took lessons. Grandfather Cantello's was our second home and I'd always march in the annual Italian-American day parade with him.

I don't think my father has read more than a dozen books in his lifetime but he'd often take me to bookstores in the area, sometimes going on into New York. We'd look at all the books on entertainers, especially on magicians. On these trips my father often talked about entertainers he'd seen and told stories about them that he'd heard. Later my mother took me to Manhattan for Arthur Godfrey broadcasts. She had a daily radio kitchen "romance" with Godfrey. Although it wasn't really intentional on their part, my parents constantly oriented me toward the stage.

But it was probably a story about America's first famous modern magician, Harry Kellar, that sent me headlong into conjuring. The incident had taken place around the turn of the century in St. George's Hall, in London, home of the world's best magic. An elaborate magician named David Devant, best of his day, performed nightly in St. George's, using effects primarily created by master technician Nevil Maskelyne. The team operated the theater, devoted entirely to magic.

Kellar had heard that Devant was practicing a form of levitation devised by Maskelyne, and took a steamer to Europe, hoping to add the effect to his already acclaimed American show. Few magicians have been able to resist attempting some form of body flotation.

Kellar was stunned, as mystified as the rest of the audience, when a lady was seen to float up gradually from a couch onstage. Apparently in a "trance," she moved away from the background of the scenery toward the center of the stage. To heighten the illusion, Devant passed a steel hoop around her body.

Night after night Kellar returned to his seat in St. George's to study the effect. Inevitably, he went backstage to offer Maskelyne a tremendous sum for the secret of his levitation technique. Maskelyne, of course, turned him down. A few nights later the frustrated Kellar jumped out of his seat and went to the front of the audience, then up on the stage, determined to discover the mechanics the British magician was employing. After an angry scene he was ushered off.

But he did bring back to New York a man named Valedon who had been an assistant to both David Devant and

23

Maskelyne. In two years Kellar had his own levitation effect and it was far more sophisticated than the incredible act that took place in St. George's Hall. He worked on a fully lit stage and climbed a ladder to pass the hoop around the subject. What struck me, reading about this at the age of nine, was the lengths to which Kellar had gone in order to create a few minutes of amazement and entertainment. He'd traveled an ocean and managed to spirit away the right-hand man of Devant and Maskelyne.

Eventually Kellar taught the illusion to Howard Thurston but there were personality clashes between them, and Kellar willed that it be sold to Harry Blackstone, another illustrious name in conjury, for the sum of one dollar (Harry Blackstone, Jr., still has the bill of sale). However, it was the Great Thurston, who died a year after I was born, who carried the levitation illusion to near ultimate. The most elaborate of all American magicians, Thurston invited people up onstage to search for wires and examine the girl as she floated. He magnanimously gave the steel hoop to an audience member, defying him to find any supports. He capped the routine with incomparable showmanship by permitting a member of the audience to touch Sleeping Beauty's ring, swearing that any wish would come true. Thurston's two- or three-hour performances were spellbinding, according to my research.

Then I began to study Houdini, who had changed his real name, Ehrich Weiss, after the great French magician Houdin. Harry Houdini was a rabbi's son who at the age of nine was a wire-act performer with Jack Hoeffler's circus. He was an escape artist, athlete, pioneering pilot and parachutist, not a formal magician. I could never get over the fact that he was afraid to drive a car. The daredevil said he was "too nervous." Although he was obsessed with exposés of trickery and illusion, Houdini still envied magicians. His act lasted only about twenty minutes and he had little else up his considerable sleeve. The brevity of his act was one reason why he took on all comers. He reaped publicity.

When one Rahmen Bey came to New York to do a "buried alive" act in a coffin onstage, surviving with very little air, Houdini quickly let it be known that he would expose the Indian "impostor." Poor Bey was reportedly baffled. A short time later Houdini was lowered into the pool of a New York hotel in a similar coffin and stayed submerged for almost an hour and a half, beating Bey's time by fifteen minutes.

Houdini then claimed that his accomplishment resulted from his "natural state," but since Rahmen Bey had been in a "trance," he was an impostor. Both men, of course, had learned to lower their metabolic rate, relax their nervous systems and not consume air. They were in exactly the same condition and not entranced. But the Houdini legend continues, as well it should. No one has come close to duplicating his feats.

What I learned from Houdini was that he often spent eighteen hours, on days that he didn't perform, perfecting his escape routines. I began to understand the time and effort necessary to go beyond simple card effects and disappearing coins.

Born too late for the golden age of magic, I tried to relive it through books. I saw Harry Blackstone perform on only two occasions and wouldn't have been more dazzled on the first occasion had Devant and Kellar been up there, too. A handkerchief, borrowed from the audience, danced all over the stage. Blackstone was smiling, master of it all. A lovely memory.

The last good American magician that I saw at work was a man named Dante. He had white hair and a white goatee, and a devilish gleam in his eyes. Indeed, he looked like Mephistopheles. He could materialize burros.

[5]

With my father, or sometimes with both our parents, Joe and I often went to Bethlehem, the rugged steel town just across the Jersey border, two hours away. My father's relatives lived in an apartment house there, occupying three of the four units. Remarkably, those not deceased still live in the same place, a big square stucco building at the foot of a high hill. Upstairs, on the left side, lived Aunt Helen and Uncle Butch Segata, a foreman at the steel mill; downstairs on the right-hand side lived Aunt Anna and her husband, John Piukutowski; over them, their son, Eddie, and daughter-in-law, Marien. As far back as I can remember, four of the family gathered each day for a game of 500-rummy. They'd shout up and down the stairs to get a game going. But as a child, I could never quite understand the peculiar Polish humor. The minute our family walked through the door, the Bethlehem relatives would yell, "Hey, when yuh goin' home?" There was much laughter in that apartment house.

Marien devoted a lot of time to me. She'd never gone to college but had read many books. She'd talk about mystery and things that couldn't be explained, and about fascinating people. She was interested in show business.

Aunt Anna was also of great influence. She was short, wore her hair in a bun, European style. Gold-rimmed glasses were perched on her nose. She had a quiet, rattling laugh that I can still hear. Ill much of the time, she couldn't get around very well, which was one reason for the daily rummy sessions.

One of my earliest memories of Aunt Anna was seeing her experimenting with a form of automatic writing. She would touch a pencil lightly to a piece of paper on a table. After a while the pencil would begin to move nervously. I couldn't have been more than six when I watched the jerky movements and Aunt Anna with a faraway look on her face.

I also remember that she once predicted that a friend of hers, one she hadn't seen or heard from in a long time, would soon pay her a visit. It was during an ouija-board session with my Aunt Helen. Five minutes later a telegram announced the impending visit of the friend. I was terribly impressed.

Aunt Anna often played with the ouija board and I was

often opposite her, later having the nerve to tell her just how it worked, which she dismissed. Once I very seriously informed her that it was an "unconscious response," a bit of brilliance extracted from my borrowed library books, interpreted one hundred percent wrong. Anna apparently took all this in stride and gladly lent herself to hours of experimentation. Eventually I did help her overcome insomnia through suggestion. I trained her to fall asleep within thirty seconds after reading a slip of paper I'd given her.

When I was in my teens, one of the best comic books ever published began to appear in the magazine section of the Caldwell drugstore a few blocks away. *Super Magician Comics* was not about Mandrake or Ibis, but about real magicians solving crimes around the world by using their illusions. Blackstone was one of them. I still have the books and cherish them.

But even before *Super Magician* came to town, I had decided to become a professional conjurer. I had put together an act; some of the effects were rather elaborate but all were home-built. Aunt Ruth Cantello had made me a tail coat, complete with inner pockets. I had tried out my act at school or at the Cantellos' or down in Bethlehem where Aunt Helen or Aunt Anna would lure as many as sixty people, usually all Polish, into the stucco apartment house for a show.

So, at ten, I began performing professionally in New Jersey, New York and Pennsylvania, billed as the "world's youngest hypnotist," an advertisement that was more come-on than truth. My "hypnotic subjects," children from the audience, were seldom cooperative. I was fumbling and awkward.

My first true "hypnotic" subject was Aunt Anna. We did a show in Bethlehem, my first before an entire adult audience, and I had her "under" in two or three minutes. I remember she was holding a pencil. I told her it was a rose. She sniffed it. Then I told her it was an onion. She made a face and tossed it away. Then I ended the demonstration by telling her that she was stuck to the chair and wouldn't be able to get up. We got great laughs and applause as she struggled to separate from the seat.

Family played an important role in the beginning. They gathered the audiences. Over in Allentown, relatives named Prorok took care of that area. In Bethlehem it worked well until too many people began showing up in the apartment house, two hundred on one occasion; then the relatives began fighting over who would sponsor the show. Finally we moved it to St. Michael's Hall, a Polish meeting place up on the hill. I performed there for a dozen straight summers.

For school performances or birthday parties, the going rate was ten or twelve dollars for a two-hour show. I pumped most if it back into props or buying effects that I couldn't build. For church performances, and I did many of them, the hat was passed with varying success—fifteen dollars the first time.

The numbers began to show some polish. I remember I tried out an effect in Helen Galloway's sixth-grade class. It was called "the Rice Bowl," a Chinese effect. China has always produced good magicians, but they've been slow in developing new effects. Until the early forties they had six basic effects, all passed down from generation to generation.

Bringing two large cereal bowls to class, I filled one to the top with rice, and then covered it with the other bowl. Shaking them, I opened them again and both bowls were overflowing with rice, spilling to the table and onto the floor. The next step was to place them together again, and on separation one would be filled with water, symbolic of China's rice and water.

I improved on the effect by filling the bowls with rice but then pulling a large bouquet of flowers instead of water from the emptied one, followed by an almost endless streamer of paper that cascaded to the floor, piling around my knees. Then I'd stop and bend over to pick it all up. Just then the streamer would begin to wriggle and I'd reach into it, pulling out my pet rabbit, Houdin.

Meanwhile, I was trying to do all sorts of things with "hypnotism," trying to mind read, collecting anything about magic or psychic experiences instead of stamps or baseball cards. Some members on my father's side of the family became alarmed at one point. I suddenly acquired a small reputation for having an "evil eye" and being able to cast a spell. I'm not sure I didn't enjoy the status, though it was kept pretty quiet.

One time I went into Baron's store in Bethlehem and bought something. After I left one of my relatives came in. The store owner complained of a headache which had started just about the time I'd entered. That mushroomed into a similar incident, and soon, in some quarters of the Polish side of the family, I was *George the Evil-Eyed*. The Polish name for it is *porabiti*. I lived it down, but to this day some of my relatives still give me strange looks.

Schoolwork was never a problem, although I wasn't a straight-A student, and Helen Galloway, now the principal of the same school, encouraged me at a time when belief in anything remotely psychic brought about a dead-fish reaction. She told me to ignore those who thought I was "odd" because I played mind games, and to keep on exploring. There was also a seventh-grade teacher, Miss Stafford, a large, dramatic woman who continued where Helen Galloway left off. One question would provoke an hour's discussion. She was fascinated with the possibility of thought perception.

Of course, magic performances continued while I was in high school, sometimes three dates a week. I performed for Boy Scout troops, Girl Scout groups, civic clubs, churches, schools —any organization willing to guarantee fifteen or twenty dollars a show. Booking myself, I ran ads in various papers, sent out mailers and prepared my own press releases. I'd outgrown the homemade tail coat, and the Bethlehem relatives, having forgiven my "evil eye," had contributed a secondhand tuxedo.

Although Joe and I always had a sibling rivalry and fought often, he was my *effects* guinea pig, lending himself to some pretty wild routines. One twilight my mother almost dropped her bag of groceries on opening the front door. Joe was levitated three or four feet off the living-room floor, sitting in a yoga position.

My mother was startled on more than one occasion. Thurston had a floating-ball illusion, sending a steel sphere around the stage and then out over the audience. Blackstone had his version. I finally worked out the mechanics of the illusion but employed a light bulb, keeping it lit and floating it around. The day I perfected it my mother happened into the dim room where I was floating the bulb, passing it back and forth through a hoop. She let out an "Eek!"

Some of my many chemistry and science experiments also created momentary upsets. I remember that an attempt to manufacture dense fog in the kitchen didn't go over too well. But each of the efforts, successes or failures, added something to the performances.

If the shows were thirty minutes, I'd work alone; if they were two hours, Joe would come along as an assistant. Looking back, I imagine they were staged as professionally as possible. To open a typical program, I'd walk out in my tuxedo, coming through the curtains carrying a cane, bowing and smiling, aping Blackstone. I'd hold the cane in front of me and change it to a silk handkerchief, shake the handkerchief and produce a bouquet of flowers. Then the curtain would open and I'd step back to the various effects tables or cabinets onstage.

One of my favorites was "the Miser's Dream," an effect often used by adult magicians. I renamed it "the Storm of Coins." Walking to the simple table in the center of the stage, I'd tap it with a wand, tossing the wand to Joe, and then produce a half dollar from my fingertips, dropping it into a pail. Rapid-fire, I'd pop about ten more, and then move offstage and into the audience, pulling coins from ear lobes and noses. Back onstage, I'd clatter thirty or forty coins into the pail, then cap the routine by changing money. Up-ending the pail, a hundred one-dollar bills would flutter out.

Turning to cards, I'd spring a deck from one hand to the other, shuffle it dramatically and then throw the cards singly into the air. They'd disappear. Tossing the rest of that deck into a top hat, I'd pop another one and begin fanning them, about twenty cards in each fan, finally doing a vanishing effect with three or four decks.

Moving quickly to more complicated illusions, I'd have someone from the audience select a card from a deck and then place it in a container given to me by a former magician named Reed who worked at the Bright Star Battery company with my father. Exposing the container so that the audience could see it, I'd burn the card and then walk to a picture frame on the other end of the stage, flinging a scarf over the frame. Returning swiftly to the container, I'd lift the lid off and whip out a half-dozen scarves. Back at the picture frame, I'd yank the scarf and expose the previously "burned" card. Striding back to the table, I'd pick up a box which had no lid or front; it was empty except for a small amount of webwork. Throwing it up, I'd catch it to reveal my rabbit nestled inside.

Usually I'd follow that effect by draping a large cloth over my shoulder, and turning back, I would produce another bouquet of flowers, all different colors. I'd freeze, do a telltale pause, tipping off the audience that something else would happen. Then I'd produce a large bowl of water; it always brought the house down.

After that, I'd do a spiritualistic thing: cause a ball to float around my shoulder and in front of me. Holding up a scarf, stretching it tight horizontally, I'd send the ball back and forth over the edge. Later on, before intermission, Joe would come out with an alarm clock and a black cloth. With the usual exaggerated gestures, I'd set the alarm and have it go off, quickly wrap the clock in the cloth and toss it all into the air. At apex, the alarm bell would stop and the cloth would fall back to the stage minus the clock.

On most shows I learned something about timing and audience communication. I began to sense the "squirmpoint." Soon I could almost feel the excitement or boredom, and would know when an illusion was not obtaining the results.

31

If the show was some distance away my father would drive us, then stand in the back of the auditorium and listen to comments. No one knew who he was, and I learned a great deal from his eavesdropping. I picked up showmanship pointers. Most entertainers could do no better than have a friend stand in the back of the room or in the lobby and just listen. After the shows we'd head back for Caldwell. My father would pass on whatever information he'd heard and then lapse into silence. We'd drive through town after town in the misty early hours of the morning. Joe often fell asleep in the back seat, which was usually crammed with equipment. He was curled around cabinets used for effects. I'll remember those rides as long as I live.

What a solid opportunity those nights offered for grounding in theater and showmanship! I can recall a very rainy night when I was a junior in high school and gave a two-hour show to raise money for the class. I was beginning a memory demonstration when one of the stand lights behind the curtain exploded. The curtain lining began to burn and white smoke enveloped me at stage center. Not aware of the fire, the audience assumed that the bang of the lamp and the smoke were some type of magical effect. I somehow remained calm and kept going with the memory demonstration while several of the stage crew extinguished the curtain and unplugged the sparking lamp. But that type of presence is unknowingly developed by repeated appearances before live audiences. One day you wake up and have it. You really don't know how you got it.

During this same period I discovered that I was more interested in audience reaction than in what I was doing onstage. It was satisfying to have the illusions work, but of greater satisfaction was the communication from beyond the footlights, the sensing of excitement, the submission to mystery. I began to realize what audience rapport meant and what it required.

In my mid-teens I was beginning to experiment constantly with ESP, attempting to perceive thoughts and plant them. My subjects were mostly fellow students. At times they would be aware of it. It reached a point, however, when I had to use caution in exercising what was becoming an acquired ability, improving yearly, in order to keep a circle of friends.

By seventeen, in my last year of high school, I was able to identify, almost immediately, any phone caller who was a personal friend. It was done automatically, without thought. I was "receiving" through hypersensitivity and telepathy. The phone would ring and I'd say, "Hi, Nancy," before Nancy Throckmorton could open her mouth. I did the same thing with Shirley Rollins, another girl friend, and several guys who were close.

Or I'd reveal thoughts at lunch break: "You're worried about that test, aren't you?" Or if the guy got a D-minus on his test and was thinking about it, I'd say, "You got a D-minus, didn't you?" I didn't realize how unnerving it was. Word got around that George Kresge was a little spooky. I untrained myself of the habit.

Earning one hundred and fifty to two hundred dollars a week now, seventy-five dollars a show, I had no thoughts of further education. I already considered myself a professional and had even worked a night club by the time I graduated from high school. My only thought was to now extend my play dates throughout the East and to the Midwest. My parents had resigned themselves to the fact that I would end my schooling in Caldwell. Then Mrs. Mary Geimer, who taught English at Caldwell High, urged me to enter college. I said that I couldn't very well do that and still keep bookings throughout the country.

"Do it part time," she said. "Just take two courses."

"Where?"

"At Seton Hall University."

It was only a half-hour from my home, famed for its

basketball team. With no more prodding than that, I enrolled in Seton Hall, with a major in psychology and a minor in Catholic philosophy.

At the same time I set about going professional all the way. I needed a stage name because I felt Kresge had little ring or flair; it also recalled the dime store and I didn't want that comparison in reviews. I thought about using my father's Polish name of Gorcza. Along with many other Poles, he'd changed his name, fearing prejudice. Yet Gorcza seemed a little heavy. Finally, from Harry Kellar I took the "k"; from the French magician Houdin, the "in," and added them to the beginning of my family name. Thus the stage name of *Kreskin*, eventually my legal name, came about.

I began to play dates in many Eastern states and the Midwest, going as far as Illinois, catching my Seton Hall classes when I could. For a while no month went by when I didn't agonize between my major and the excitement of performing. There was also the religious issue. I'm a good Catholic, I think, and at the time my "hypnosis" work was at some odds with the Church. There was controversy within the Church about the controlling of the will of a human being. Great stress was placed on the necessity of having freedom of will. Earlier I'd considered becoming a priest. Catholic philosophy deeply ingrained in me, I struggled with the question for several years, then reached my own decision: *I was not controlling will.* "Hypnosis" is not capable of it.

My routine now featured "hypnosis." I sent a mailer to six or seven hundred colleges and slowly began to travel the college circuit. I also worked night clubs, private parties, conventions. Yet, because of my age, twenty then, it was sometimes hard for me to realize I was a pro. After a fraternal-organization reunion performance, I met an executive from All-State Insurance Company. He asked, "What do you charge?" I told him my usual fee was seventy-five dollars for an hour program; one hundred dollars for an hour and a half; for a two-hour show, one hundred and twenty-five dollars. He said, "When my company calls you, tell them four hundred dollars."

I couldn't bring myself to do it. I played many dates for All-State but never charged more than one hundred and fifty dollars.

I finally broke this hang-up in 1956. Barbara Hamilton, a girl I knew, called to book me into St. Lawrence University in Canton, New York. She told me that they always had a "hypnotist" appear. She named one. "How much does he get?" I asked. The answer was five hundred dollars. "I want the same," I said bluntly. I'd now been "hypnotizing" for more than ten years, and believed I had a better show than Performer X. The university refused, but the next year I played there for a single show at my new price. At last I had reached what I thought was "big time." I felt much older than twenty, yet knew I wasn't. It all had come about so slowly that it seemed there had been no changes since those nights riding with my father and Joe. There had been many, in fact, and my work was imperceptibly changing from magic to ESP.

Meanwhile, I was a serious student of psychology whenever I could get a few days in a row to attend Seton Hall. The university, particularly Professor Frank Murphy, made allowances for the time factor but not the course credits. It took me nine and a half years to graduate.

My thesis was entirely practical. I spent months in research on the use of suggestion to improve bowling scores. One bowler I worked with raised her average by twenty-seven points, so it wasn't a total loss. I'm still not certain why I selected this subject instead of a more clinical area. One reason, I'm sure, is that I could evaluate the results by "points" rather than by theory.

[6]

One man is often responsible for the difference between a performer wallowing around on the bottom, begging for chances and eventually giving up, or going to the top of whatever he does best. I found that man in the unlikely person of Louis Reda, an office-equipment dealer from the small town of Easton, Pennsylvania. He sells typewriters and desks during the times he isn't booking me, checking contracts or attending to the details of concerts in Boston one night, Sioux Falls the next. In ten years' association, we've never had a contract. It's unorthodox, almost a family affair. His wife, Timmi, does my banking across from their office.

Lou first turned me over to a pair of typical talent agents. They were mostly verbal, which is typical too. Lou then stepped in, and without experience but with considerable shrewdness and bald honesty, began to plot a course. Since I wasn't well known, Lou decided we should try for the talk shows on TV. We drove to New York and went to the Les Crane people at ABC. I did some card effects, but the Crane staff didn't show much interest. We returned to Easton, slightly dejected, but decided to try again, this time with the new *Merv Griffin Show*.

On that venture, for some odd reason, neither Lou nor I fully appreciated the fact that it was a legal holiday in New York. We found the Griffin offices practically deserted. But lights were on in one cubbyhole. The occupant was Tom O'Malley, a member of Griffin's staff. He seemed amused that we'd picked a holiday to go job hunting, and agreed to listen. He wanted to know what I did.

"Is there anyone else around?" I asked, pulling out a deck of cards. "A secretary," O'Malley answered.

"Would you please call her and ask her to think of any card in the deck?"

O'Malley shrugged and picked up the phone. I placed a card from the pack beside the phone.

In a moment the girl responded and O'Malley peered down at the card, face up, on his desk. I'd hit it.

He said, "I'll be damned," and looked at Lou and me. "I may get in touch with you," he added.

36

A few days later we went back to the *Les Crane Show*, and again there seemed to be mixed interest. While we were there, a call came from Tom O'Malley, who'd once been associated with the zany *Candid Camera* program, I learned later. He was accustomed to wild things.

Lou took the call, talked for a minute, then hung up, saying to me, "Let's go." We started to exit.

The Crane people, rather puzzled, asked, "Where are you going?" We hadn't finished talking to them.

Lou answered, hardly concealing his delight, "To the *Merv Griffin Show*. We're on in two hours."

Next we went to Philadelphia to see some of the *Mike Douglas Show* staff members. They required auditions for everyone not known to them, but we told Roger Ayles and Larry Rosen that no meaningful audition could be held for an ESP experiment. It would require an audience. They gambled and I went on the Douglas show within two weeks. Eighty-odd Douglas appearances later, I'm still impressed with the Ayles-Rosen decision to take a chance on a mentalist who dropped in from nowhere, in tow of an office-equipment salesman.

[7]

Any performer is terrified of failure before an audience. Anyone in my field is particularly terrified of it because of the skepticism and constant challenging of the house. A juggler misses an Indian club and everyone shrugs it off, but it is something else with a mentalist. The word itself rightfully challenges an audience. The ball park is the human mind and anyone can play. Occasionally, at the beginning of a program, I can feel the skepticism. Yet, after skepticism is overcome, the audience will go the other way and root for success.

If I fail in a theater or night club, I will repeat the experiment. Time allows this luxury. Television, however, affords few mistakes. And, too, failure before a thousand people is bad enough; before a million it's a personal and professional nightmare. I had my nightmare with a large Mosler safe.

When a subject is locked in a safe onstage, with knowledge of the combination, concentrating on the sequence of numbers, I receive them in separated units—the usual composition of a combination—rather than in blocks. No image is projected in this case. Of course, the speed with which I receive them and then unlock the safe depends entirely on the person inside. Usually, after a few seconds in that hot darkness, they begin communicating. I can feel the urgency.

I first did this routine on my own syndicated TV show in Ottawa, borrowing a large safe from the Chubb, Mosler, Taylor Company, plus an expert. Initially I wanted to go the limit: have no other person on earth know the combination except the man imprisoned inside, and no safety factors. My proposed subject, Herman Steebs, was willing. He said he'd seen me work before and had no doubt that I could release him. Since he was a quiet, calm man, I had the feeling that he would not panic and consume larger amounts of air.

However, I then began to seriously consider the natural "air time" within the safe, estimated at roughly fifteen minutes, as well as the fact that I might have misjudged the subject and that he might faint or have a heart attack. The other possibility, of course, was that I'd keel over. We finally decided to impose two safety factors: a mechanic would be standing by with a high-powered drill, and Steebs would give the combination to the police station, sealed in an envelope. We'd then hook a "red phone" to the main station, enabling an instant call for help if we needed it. I admit the latter was planned as suspense showmanship rather than a rigid safety factor. However, as these things sometimes go, we did need to make a call.

Cameras rolling, Steebs got into the safe and the door clanged shut. I spun the tumbler to lock it. Steebs heard my rap on the safe and began communicating the units of the combination. I noticed immediately that he seemed icy calm though in a hunched position in absolute darkness within three-inch steel walls. In my mind I could see him and felt tremendous admiration. Consuming little air, he was not panicking. He was clicking off the numbers with precision.

I bent over and began following him. Right. Left. BACK. Right again. Back again. Two more units and he ended it. I expected to hear the click, pull the door dramatically, and expose him as a human sardine. Nothing. No click. I started the sequence of numbers again. Steebs was still sending strongly.

I spun the numbers out a second time, making certain I hit every mark. No click.

Meanwhile, in the control booth, a member of my staff heard another man from the safe company say, "He has it wrong." Under pressure, Steebs had divulged the units to this associate. I suppose the company was skeptical.

I tried a third time, then a fourth and fifth. Finally I stood up, my mouth getting a little dry. We were now about six minutes into the experiment. Remarkably, Steebs was remaining calm and I sent strongly, telling him that everything was all right. Far from it.

The other gentleman came out of the control booth and tried the tumbler, using the exact units that I had received. He had no success. It was now evident that there was a malfunction in the locking device and we summoned the mechanic. As he began work on the safe door, I picked up the red phone to call for additional help. Some eight minutes had been consumed—past the halfway mark of available air. The police switchboard was busy.

As I stood back, no longer the star of the show—the man with the drill had taken over that role—I wondered why in heaven's name I'd ever tried the silly routine. But I've never been so grateful, nor humble, standing before the talents of a man with a drill.

In a few minutes the door of the safe was literally dismantled, and Steebs crawled out. He showed some signs of chagrin that it hadn't worked, and was slightly flushed from the heat within the safe. Otherwise, he was in good shape—great performance on his part. A post-mortem revealed that he had sent the correct combination, and that I had received it. Examination of the tumbler showed that it had been jarred in moving the safe from the stage to the platform. The safety factor we'd all forgotten was to have Mr. Steebs check the steel box after it had been put in position.

One of my rules for the TV program is to always show the failures as well as the successes. We had kept the cameras running throughout the entire period, eleven minutes or so, but it did not seem fair to the safe expert or to myself to call this a failure. ESP had worked, the tumbler had not. So we decided to shelve the footage and do it again. Five weeks later we were successful within six minutes. This time no person on earth knew the combination except Steebs, and we didn't have to use the red phone.

There are also occasions when failure is only a hand movement away. Using twenty-two directories, I did the telephone-book demonstration with singer Pearl Bailey on the *Mike Douglas Show*. Writing a name on notepaper, I shoved it into an envelope and passed it to Douglas; then I directed Miss Bailey to open one of the directories, instructing her verbally to choose any book she liked. *Nonverbally, by telepathic suggestion alone,* I ordered her to choose Albuquerque, which she did.

Holding the phone book over one arm, I began thumbing pages until she said "Stop." I glanced and saw that she'd stopped on the page I had in mind. Thus far, it was working. On the right-hand page was the name I'd written out and given to Douglas. Actually, there were two names of that identical spelling, in small type, separated by no more than a crochet-needle tip.

I then asked Pearl to close her eyes and circle her fingertip over both pages and "come down anywhere you want." At the same time I was pinpointing, by mental suggestion, the specific name. Her reactions until then had been so spontaneous and correct that I felt nothing could go wrong. Her finger jabbed down, very hard, and I turned ashen as I realized that she'd hit the left page. There was no such name on that page. But then her hand bounced and slid over to the right-hand page, finger ending exactly on the name Douglas held in the envelope.

Obviously the mental impressions she'd received were strong enough to overcome my lack of judgment in suggesting that she use the area of both pages to select the crucial name. However, before cameras at a time like this, you are not analytical—just paralyzed.

During the first commercial break on that same show, Pearl mentioned to Douglas and myself that she planned to write her life story but had never taken the time, and that a publisher was interested. On another commercial break she unexplainably rose and walked out into the studio audience of about a hundred and fifty people. Stepping over legs, she placed her hands on one man's shoulders, saying, "Man, oh, man, I don't know why I'm doing this."

It turned out that her publisher had sent his representative to the Douglas show, hopeful of talking with her. Out of the entire audience, she'd picked the one person who had something important to discuss with her. Because she is a show-business person, an extrovert, impulsive and spontaneous, she'd responded to his thoughts. It is an excellent example of everyday, nontheatrical ESP.

[8]

As any current performer well knows, television consumes material at a pace that leaves you breathless, and there is a constant search for new routines or conversion of old routines. In my case, the twist is to find a mental application.

For instance, I sometimes duplicate the drawing of a guest artist or cartoonist who is hidden from me by a screen, picking up the mental image. This is done with the artist working some eight or ten feet away at an easel with a sketch pad, his back to the audience. In a similar position, I also have a sketch pad. I mentally "see" his pencil or charcoal as he begins to draw lines, provided he is concentrating deeply on what he is drawing. My own sketch, a very rough approximation because I have no talent as an artist, is delayed by thirty seconds or so. I mentally and crudely copy as best I can.

The applications are practically endless and it's fun to come up with new ones. On one TV show the guest star was to be Betsy Palmer, who happens to be a marvelous cook as well as a fine actress and panelist. I requested that she bake a cake and bury a personal object in it. The cake would then be placed in one of twelve identical "bakery" boxes. With the help of her concentration I was to select the right box and then identify the object buried beneath the frosting.

For some reason on that particular day I could not select the target box, although Betsy, as usual, was coming through in definite terms. I simply couldn't read her in this phase. At last she pointed to the problem container and then began concentrating on the object within the cake. I soon got the impression that "crying" was attached to it, then found my way to finally describe it as a baby tooth. Betsy cut the cake, and the tooth, which had belonged to her daughter, causing some weeping on its loss, was again extracted.

I seek out credible experiments which are interesting, I hope, as well as visual. On another show I had actor Robert Horton, a star of *Wagon Train* and other TV dramas, take a Polaroid shot of a member of the audience and leave it in the camera, undeveloped. Horton's instructions were to snap the picture while the person was entering the studio. My job was to identify the person by perceiving Bob's thoughts; final proof being the developed picture.

At one point in the program Horton sat on the stage, camera in his lap, and concentrated on the person. I decided his subject had been female, as I was receiving a description of a person in a "red dress." I went out into the audience and asked a number of ladies in red dresses to please stand. I touched one lady in red several times but got negative responses from Horton. As I stood before a girl, my back to Horton, I got an extremely positive response. I said, "Your picture is in Mr. Horton's camera." Bob pulled the tab on the Polaroid and while we waited for the development I asked the young lady to concentrate on her name. I was able to get it, and then Horton presented her with a candid shot of herself walking into the studio in Ottawa.

I constantly try to come up with something that will have ESP applications, yet be mainly visual and, hopefully, exciting. At one production meeting, producer Dick Reid said, "Do you think you could do something physical? Really dramatic. Life or death."

Flippantly I said, "Maybe I could hang myself."

Everyone laughed.

However, I began to think about it, and being a Houdini buff, decided it wasn't such a bad idea after all. I liked the idea of life depending on a simple mental direction.

We talked about it and then sketched it out. Finally we choreographed it to have five nooses on a scaffold of which one would be connected with a rope only stapled to the top crosspiece. I selected number 4 as the innocent noose. The other nooses would be firmly secured and entirely lethal. If I was correctly guided to the stapled rope it would pull free when I jumped. If the directions were false, I would have a very sore neck, if not a broken one.

Reid then lined up Tom Tryon, actor turned best-selling author with his chilling *The Other*, as the telepathic guide to life or death.

We constructed the scaffolding and got an expert to fashion the five nooses. Next, the crew filled four bags with 155 pounds (my weight) of sand, and painted markers with the numbers 1 to 5.

When I first saw the scaffolding with the five nooses hanging down, I felt a great temptation to call the whole thing off.

Instead, I phoned my doctor to fly up to Canada for the show. Dr. Robert Stein wasn't of much comfort when he examined the nooses and said, "If you don't get the right one, you'll fall two feet. That's enough to snap your neck unless you're relaxed." Relaxed?

The nooses were set with eight inches of slack so that the sandbags would jerk realistically.

Tryon arrived that night and I told him he was to select one of the numbered markers by impulse, by obeying whatever thought came into his mind. Not to reason—just to pick! We would have no verbal communication once the routine started until he commanded me to jump. My role was to make certain he picked the harmless noose. They all looked the same.

Several hours later cameras began rolling and we eventually came to the "Hangman's Noose" slot in the program. The scaffolding was wheeled out and chairs placed beneath the five nooses. It was dramatic-looking, to say the least.

I was then tightly blindfolded and began mental communication with Tryon, ordering him to select the number 4 marker, none other. He made his choice, but I did not know what number he was holding. At this time his directions to the crew were silent. He was pointing to the other chairs to have them occupied with the sandbag dummies. They were quickly tied to the nooses.

Tryon then led me to chair number 4, which I mounted. I still did not know that it was the correct chair beneath the stapled noose. The crew slipped the noose around my neck and tightened it.

Tryon then directed the crew to kick out one of the chairs. I felt the thump of the sandbag and heard the chair clatter simultaneously. The whole scaffolding shuddered as the rope jerked 155 pounds.

Another chair was kicked out. That sickening thud and scaffold jarring came again. Then the third sandbag fell and I could scarcely breathe. If I was standing on the wrong chair . . .

Two were left.

I heard him say, "Kreskin."

I jumped and the rope pulled out easily. Even then, I got a slight rope burn from the noose.

Happily, I had both feet on the stage when they kicked the last chair away. I now have the feeling that if given a choice, I'd prefer a gas chamber. There is something about standing there with a noose around your throat that defies adequate description.

Perception of numbers is perhaps the easiest ESP effect to attain because a mathematical logic is inherent; communication is limited to an arrangement of digits. They are comparatively easy to send, require no great thought process for the subject and are therefore less difficult to receive. Numbers, after all, are among the first things we learn as children.

Complications are apt to set in quickly once the 1-2-3's and A-B-C's are left behind. Even so, the simple beginnings are preferable. At a Vegas Hilton show I kept receiving a set of initials and finally the subject arose. He appeared to be a gentleman in his late fifties. I was able to identify the initials and it opened his mind. I then worked my way to identify that they belonged to his son. He was still receptive, and I went deeper with him. He sent strongly.

"Your son is in the military," I said. "Is it the Army?"

"Yes."

He did not want to stop. I said, "You want him to be a general."

The man smiled. "He's on the promotion list."

And we ended it.

But the gentleman had come through clearly on each step beyond the three-letter beginning, although I hadn't been able to read which branch of the military his son served. "Army" was a guess.

Audience participation routines are apt to be loaded with surprises and my particular brand invites ulcers. During a concert for U.S. Steel in Chicago's McCormick Hall, a man suddenly stood up and wanted to ask a question. I was annoyed. He'd interrupted a train of thought. There is a definite factor of control in a mentalism performance, and he had "targeted" in, which was my role.

I fought back the annoyance mainly because he was plunging ahead before I could interrupt. He said he was a doctor and had diagnosed an illness that afternoon. Could I tell him what the diagnosis was? Plainly, he was testing me. It was a cold challenge. Had he not been a doctor, I probably would have found a way to seat him politely. The fact that he was a physician, a psychiatrist for all I knew, would have cast doubt on the rest of the performance. I decided to try.

"I don't have a medical background, so please think of the letters, not the word," I said, crossing all sorts of fingers. Undoubtedly, it would be one of those long Latin names that I couldn't have pronounced, much less spelled.

He concentrated and I received them, one by one, writing down twenty-one letters on the blackboard. I was incorrect on one, but considerably relieved that I'd accepted his challenge. The show soared.

Both the intruding doctor and the Army officer's father were excellent subjects but some people cannot respond, though they might like to, in setting up communication for either thought perception or suggestibility. They are concerned about opening up "mental closets." Another barrier is that they will have to concentrate with a total stranger. I appreciate the reluctance. But this inability is not as common as one might think. Maybe one person in twenty, an exceedingly low figure, is unable to respond to even the slightest degree.

Certain personality factors seem to enter into the "shut mind" person. The bullheaded, narrow-minded person always has trouble; the creative person is often the perfect subject. In suggestibility, a safer area than thought perception, almost everyone can respond to some degree. Some cannot respond on the stage but will freely follow suggestion in private. Others respond better in groups because of the security in numbers. In both categories, for obvious reasons, children are the best subjects. They aren't set in their ways; their imagination is more open.

In these communications I think that the subject is only aware of a slight effort, though he may be concentrating very hard. But it is not like pumping a bicycle up a hill. Attention has been gained; he or she is conditioned. The subject is gradually harnessed to the point where there is full participation—automatic response without great awareness.

Almost nightly, things do occur that aren't programmed at all. I will receive a message that isn't really intended but is strong enough to carry. In the Playboy Club in Baltimore, I broke a train of thought with: "Someone is looking for the rest of a twenty-dollar bill." One of the Bunnies almost dropped her tray.

Later I found out that she'd just come from the kitchen and had seen half of a twenty-dollar bill lying on the floor. Who wouldn't be intrigued or have their thoughts completely arrested? As she came back into the club she was naturally puzzled, occupied with the whereabouts of that other half. Everything but one subject had been cleared from her mind. To me, "psyched up," mentally listening for any signal, it couldn't have been stronger if she'd shouted it.

At the Westbury Music Fair, on New York's Long Island, I found myself bombarded by a thought of "hair." Someone seemed to be concentrating on "treating hair" or "fixing" it. I mentioned the subject and then immediately went into some detail. I noticed that a girl who was seated near the front got up and hurriedly left the theater. Obviously there was a connection. Several hours later I was introduced to her. She was secretary to Lee Gruber, owner of the theater, and had been discussing, with a friend seated next to her, plans to open a beauty salon. They'd talked for about ten minutes pre-show and her thoughts had carried over into my opening minutes.

She certainly hadn't expected me to perceive them, which is why she'd become startled and bolted out.

In another, very different circumstance I cut short a performance at the Embers Club in Indianapolis because I was receiving something very troubling from a lady in the audience. I didn't attempt to go into the problem, or what I thought the problem might be, because I'm not a minister or doctor. I did manage to pick her out at a table—or I made a guess that she was the person. She kept staring at me with anxiety. So I cut the show by about twenty minutes and left the spotlight.

Locating Bob Kaytes, I asked him to have his wife strike up a conversation with the woman and attempt to bring her backstage. After a few minutes they arrived in my dressing room, and in another few minutes my hunch was confirmed. She admitted that she was planning suicide. People who are thinking of it are usually seeking help but can't put it into words. The Kayteses arranged for assistance.

[9]

Hopeful of spontaneity, praying for something offbeat to happen, aside from personal problems, I never know exactly what I'm going to do or how the experiment will turn out.

During one Johnny Carson show, with singer Jack Jones and comedienne Marilyn Michaels appearing as guests, I decided to switch the format. I was scheduled to do a "chalk writing" demonstration—cause a piece of chalk between two slates to write a telepathically received name—and had written out some one hundred and fifty names on the backs of calling cards—Flip Wilson, Peter Nero, Henry Mancini and others. Jones and Miss Michaels were to select a card, concentrate on that particular name, and my role was to perceive it, then cause the chalk to write the name. We'd planned to do four or five names.

However, glancing at the clock, I realized we were running

late and could not cover more than one or two names. I decided it would be more dramatic to have Miss Michaels think of a name, any name, and then proceed with the balance of the test.

I took the two black slates, which had been wiped clean, and gave them to the guests. After soaking a piece of chalk in a glass of water, to make certain I'd get an impression, I inserted the chalk between the slates. They were then tightly bound with elastic. While Jones and Miss Michaels held them parallel over the floor, I told Marilyn to think of someone she knew that no one else in the studio audience would be likely to know. In particular, it would be someone I could not possibly know.

Marilyn soon nodded and informed Jones of the name. They began to concentrate.

I experienced considerable difficulty because the name was very complex. "Mentally spell it, please," I requested. Finally getting what I thought to be the name, I proceeded to the third sequence of the effect, which was to manipulate the chalk, make it write, even though I was seven or eight feet away from the slates.

As Jones removed the elastic and opened the two slates, I was relieved to see that the chalk had rolled and the name "Oishe" was spelled out. Again, I'd had that fear of failure when a TV camera is focused in close.

Marilyn was visibly shaken, almost hysterical. The program shifted to a commercial, so she could gather herself together. Moishe Oishe, her uncle, a famous cantor, had been dead since the forties. Only Marilyn, within the studio, could have been thinking about him.

This impromptu demonstration was an example of energy force, but not psychokinesis, in which objects are moved by sheer mental will force. The chalk writing is an effect, and I label it as such.

Another example of this occurred on the *Merv Griffin Show*. Before I'm accused of name-dropping, I cite these examples because they were performed in full public view, with known and reputable persons involved, in this case a dozen or so people, Griffin to technicians, in close observation.

The participants were vocalist Della Reese and the husband-wife team of Eli Wallach and Anne Jackson. I selected Anne and Della as the subjects, asking Della to tear out some cigarette papers from a roll-your-own folder, then press them into tiny balls. After she'd arranged them on the coffee table, I instructed her to pick up one of them and place it in the palm of her hand, then close the palm tightly.

Turning to Anne Jackson, I asked her to concentrate on some famous person in American history, and that the person be deceased. I often make the latter request to avoid names in current news.

In a moment I received her impression and said, "Anne, you seem to be picturing this person sitting down." I told her several times that he appeared to be confined in something.

She nodded, startled.

Then I received the total image. "The person you're picturing is in late life and ill. He's Franklin D. Roosevelt."

With that registered, I told Della to unroll the tiny ball of paper she was holding and to dust cigarette ashes over it. That took a few seconds. Then she shrieked, and the camera moved in for a close-up of "FDR" formed in ashes on the crumpled paper.

At this point, I can understand a reader reaction of "Hold it, by limiting the famous person to the deceased, you narrow your field; you could have tricked or pre-treated the paper." Possibly, but that would mean tricking papers for perhaps fifty thousand deceased persons from Washington and Patrick Henry and John Paul Jones to Eisenhower and John Kennedy. I'd have to lug a truckload of cigarette papers from perform-ance to performance. And on any given day or night a subject would pop an odd-ball "Jesse James's brother Frank" on me, for which I hadn't prepared a paper. Truthfully, I can't think of a more complicated way to accomplish five minutes of entertainment.

Yet I've found that I cannot resist this type of "before your very eyes" effect. I'm as much a fan of them as anyone in a simon-pure audience. When I see a new one, I gasp and react with the same "How was that done?"

In the thirties there was a very creative effects inventor named Samuel C. Hooker. He wasn't a professional magician but was perhaps the first true scholar of sorcery. He conceived an effect in which cards would rise, on command, from a drinking glass or goblet. Initially magicians scoffed at it but then he invited fifteen or twenty to his home, suggesting that they bring their own decks of cards. Not only did Dr. Hooker permit them to shuffle their own decks but confidently told them to mark certain cards by writing their names on them. Placing the deck in a drinking glass, he ordered specific cards to rise, then capped it by having the owner's "name" card pop up. For his encore Dr. Hooker placed the glass beneath a bell jar so that nothing could be attached to the deck. Walking away, he "spoke" to one or more cards and up they came.

After researching this feat for years I finally got it to work, then put an ESP twist on it. I ask three different people in the audience to think of a card each from one deck but to remain silent as to the selection. They are requested to concentrate on their card.

I hand another deck to a lady down front, a volunteer, and then escort her to the stage. She deposits that deck into the goblet which is on a table. I then leave the stage and join the audience.

As I receive the impression from the first person, the card he or she has in mind rises. The second subject is requested to concentrate deeply. I ask the volunteer on stage to please squeeze the goblet. The second card rises.

At this point I return to the stage and enclose the goblet in a bell jar, thanks to Dr. Hooker's pioneering. I request the third person to concentrate, then walk away about twenty paces, finally turning indignantly to shout, "Rise, card."

I think I get a bigger bang out of it than the audience when the card pops up.

All of these demonstrations are attempts to show energy forces at work, though none of them are accomplished by purely psychological means. Legitimate scientific principles involving physical movement are used. For instance, the cigarette papers are never tricked or pre-treated. I've offered them for chemical analysis. Of the three demonstrations, the chalk writing is by far the most complicated. It is a controlled situation, similar to the card levitation and the ash effect, but much more elaborate.

I have to laugh when someone targets the water as the key to the chalk effect. The water is simply to ensure an impression of the chalk. It becomes saturated and sticky after it is dropped into the glass. I can't gamble on hard chalk to write one hundred percent of the time.

As the slates are held parallel over the floor by the two participants, there is a natural tendency for hand movement. No human hand can hold an object perfectly still; there is always a slight nervous reaction. I take complete advantage of this mobile state to guide their writing—"Oishe" in this instance. I cause the chalk to write the thought that is in their minds by control of their hands. The two participants never physically touch the chalk. It is a mixture of thought perception, suggestibility and natural physical force.

These particular demonstrations are plainly labeled as effects and removed, in a way, from the straight parapsychology portions of the shows or concerts. An entertainer must be, or should be, versatile. I attempt to be.

Table tilting or table moving is supposedly straight out of the séance setting and medium's bag of tricks, or some people claim that it is a psychokinetic manifestation. Unfortunately, perhaps for me, I've never seen what I would consider to be absolute proof of movement of an *inanimate, brainless* object by mental force alone. It may occur, but I just haven't been around when it has happened. More than that, I've tried very hard to move ashtrays and wastebaskets and even feathers by sheer mental will force. So far, I've not been able to move anything by so-called pure psychokinetic force. Yet I've tilted and moved tables on my own show, the *David Frost Show*, and on Johnny Carson's stage. No psychokinesis, or telekinesis or teleportation, as it is also termed, is involved.

I usually employ one or more card tables, light but strong. The hands of the four subjects at each table are placed firmly on the top, palms down, with the right little finger touching the left little finger of the person to the right, the reverse with the opposite hand. In that way, there is magnetic and dynamic contact between all four persons. On signal, the tables often move so violently that the sitters have to stand up; the tables actually travel. One fell into an orchestra pit; another went through the rear curtain backdrop with all four participants racing with it. In Dallas, at the University of Texas, I remember that the card table supplied me was flimsy and kept collapsing. It can be a very funny routine—ten tables dancing almost simultaneously, forty people with open mouths. Yet it is a legitimate phenomenon.

On the Carson show, the table rammed Johnny's desk; on the Frost show, two of the four tables flipped over. Frost became so interested in the dancing tables that he stopped the flow of other guests to question the participants. One girl said she felt "moving water on the table top." A man said that it seemed as if "electricity was in the table." Others said that their hands seemed to "go numb."

Table tilting is based on the dynamic responses of the nervous system to thought and is not remotely supernatural or mediumistic. The effect is akin to the action of the ouija board and in the family of automatic writing, not even a distant cousin to psychokinesis. The table tilts or moves as the result of automatic responses in our nervous systems triggered by mental concentration. Eight hands build up stresses to accomplish this strange phenomenon. Each person knows what he wants to happen; each concentrates physically. It was once described to me as a "chemical neuromuscular" response, requiring physical contact which is the separation point for so-called psychokinesis.

The Phoenix, a magician's magazine of the forties, relates a story of eight magicians who questioned the phenomenon, believing that table tilting was a fake. (It can be phony, but there is no reason for it.) They gathered in New York City and sat at a heavy oaken table for an hour. The whole table went over.

For party fun, any four people can tilt tables all over the place. Best results demand firm contact of the palms on the card-table surface: physical contact with the partners, little fingers touching, and then some patience. First tries may take thirty minutes. I speed up the process with my subjects through suggestibility.

Similarly, automatic writing is often draped in the phony garments of the occult and placed in séance rooms. To bring it into true light the reader of this book may practice automatic writing. It requires sitting down for five minutes a day for a few weeks with a pencil in the writing hand, be it right or left. Let the pencil rest lightly on a piece of paper and clear the mind by thinking of something far removed. Attempt to make it unaware of the pencil or pad—daydream if possible. It may not work the first few days simply because not all people can "clear their minds" without some conditioning. Do not try to make the mind a "blank." It cannot be done. But sooner or later the pencil will move, and automatically.

At first the pencil may only make simple lines or zigzags. Continued sessions, however, will produce letters. They will run together, since the pencil is not lifted. Additional sessions will eventually bring words, responses from the unconcious telegraphed to the paper without guided thought. On rare occasions the transcription will be reversed, necessitating a mirror. It is a strange phenomenon and the people who "mirror-write" seem to do it consistently.

In contrast to this legitimate area of mental-dynamic energy I have, for effect, "levitated" objects in recent years, after abandoning magic. Not long ago I requested two female volunteers to place their hands on a rather heavy French table, along with mine. We appeared to "levitate" the table across the stage and down into the audience. There were no wires or hooks, and it was not a trick table. I requested the audience to examine it. However, it was a physical, not psychological, technique.

Though I now create visual illusions as much for self-amusement as for the stage, some take years to perfect. I work on them at odd times, finding it fun. "Ball and Goblet," dating back to my wind-up years as a magician, is in that category—it took fifteen years. Visually, the concept is simple but the mechanics are complex. I constructed an oblong wooden box with the front side open and exposed if a small draw curtain was not pulled. Placing a sponge rubber ball against the left wall of the box, I put an ordinary champagne goblet upright against the opposite wall. The goal was to persuade the ball to travel across the floor of the box and hop up into the goblet.

Since 1957 I'd had more failures than successes with it but in 1972 I finally made a public test at the Phillipsburg Catholic High School in New Jersey. Prior to that morning performance I practiced in my manager's home from about 1 A.M. to 6 A.M., final rehearsal of some two hundred. Three or four times I made the ball move a few inches. Once I found it inexplicably at the back, lodged up between the cabinet wall and the goblet. However, I persuaded it to hop into the glass four times and decided I was ready to try it before the high school seniors. The ball performed.

Having "tried out" in Phillipsburg, I packed the cabinet and flew to Ottawa. Sheila Ostrander and Lynn Schroeder, authors of a fascinating book entitled *Psychic Discoveries behind the*

Iron Curtain, were to be special guests on that particular taping, so I decided to use them as witnesses and assistants. Requesting them to examine the cabinet, which was placed on a sheet of glass between two chairs, I also asked them to check the ball to eliminate the possibility of an electronic device being hidden within, and to search for wires or other physical attachments. After a moment they seemed satisfied.

I was standing about ten feet away. Sheila drew the small curtain on the cabinet and I counted to five, at which time she pulled the curtain again. I noticed that the ball had literally crawled about three inches, then stopped; the goblet was empty.

If an effect doesn't work on TV, I usually move on to something else due to the time factor. But on this occasion I couldn't bring myself to abandon years of effort in five seconds. I asked producer Dick Reid if we could try again and keep the cameras rolling. He agreed. This time the ball behaved.

Later Miss Ostrander said, "Come on, Kres, how'd you do it?"

Someone standing nearby said, "The curtain did it."

I stepped back. One of the oldest ploys in magic is to entrap the witness by providing a logical explanation for the effect or illusion, then shatter the explanation. (Thurston and Blackstone were masters at it.) I proceeded to dismantle the entire cabinet in five seconds, demonstrating the total absence of gimmickry.

Others have gone to their graves with certain effects and I hope to go to mine with a few. I don't refuse information simply to annoy people, but having spent time perfecting several special *physical* entertainment techniques, such as linking of finger rings from the audience, I'll go to a point in discussing them and then stop. Where illusion and effects are concerned, I'd rather leave an audience steeped in mystery. Also, there is a guardianship that stems from early conjuring, an overwhelming desire to provoke that irresistible *"Aah"* from the audience. It's heady.

One of Houdini's greatest escape tricks was "the Chinese Water Torture Cabinet." He was hung upside down, in stocks, in a cabinet containing water. It resembled a coffin, upended, with a glass front. Plunged down into it, he could only survive on the air that was in his lungs. The curtains were closed and a moment later he appeared onstage, dripping and bowing. Along with others, I studied this effect for years. Finally I discovered the methodology he used to escape the Puritan stocks and then open the outer padlock on the coffin. Eventually I was able to obtain a copy of the original plans of the cabinet. Only two or three sets exist, to my knowledge, and I treasure mine. Many of Houdini's effects defied solution long after his death. Thankfully, his assistants refused to reveal the methods. In time I'll probably do a variation of the Chinese Water Torture Cabinet, keying it to an ESP application.

Leaving most performers gasping, television devours both talent and material nightly, constantly forcing new applications. Even night clubs and college circuits place great demands on material. The entertainer who repeats himself year after year soon faces a diminishing audience, although the public usually demands his specialties or trademarks. The only solution is yearly development of additional effects, twists on past applications.

Polishing touches are now being put on a new one in which a member of the audience will extract a coin from his pocket and concentrate on the date. If I perceive it correctly, it will appear on the bottom of a soot-coated tin lid held by a volunteer on stage; another volunteer will pass a candle flame back and forth under the lid to register the date. It is, admittedly, a variation of the "cigarette paper" effect, combining thought perception with a visual denouement. Few effects are entirely new. But by 1975 I hope I will have discarded it for something more unique.

[10]

When communication is without sound, darkness seems to present an added barrier. I have perceived thoughts with the audience and stage completely blacked out, but for reasons unknown, perhaps psychological, the communication is always easier when the sender can see me. It may be the security of visual contact. We aren't moles by nature.

I first tried thought perception while blindfolded on the *Mike Douglas Show.* It was a new and not altogether pleasant sensation. I was telepathically directed by commedienne Moms Mabley to follow a circuitous route toward a balloon held by someone in the audience, a version of "Pin the Tail on the Donkey." I managed to puncture the balloon on the first try but en route almost fell over a camera. Moms forgot to warn me. I was moving rather quickly.

I've also been successful at going out into an audience blindfolded to select twins seated separately while the parents were concentrating onstage. Although I've never tried it, I think this guidance would be much more difficult if the parents were blindfolded too, and simply gave me row and seat references.

I do not think that telepathy can work readily with an unseen total stranger—perhaps someone in the adjoining hotel room. It would be a major breakthrough if I'm proved wrong. But I'm inclined to believe that a brief moment to establish rapport is necessary. It could be accomplished on the phone or with a few seconds of both visual and verbal contact.

As an example of this, I did an interview on the *John Wingate Show* over New York's radio station WOR. During the interview an engineer left the booth and came into the studio, and we chatted for a moment. Returning to the booth, he wrote a word on a slip of paper, then began concentrating on it. In my mike position, I could neither see nor hear him, yet was able to pick up the word in about thirty seconds. We'd had that brief moment of rapport.

I cannot, nor do I try to, perceive the thoughts of anyone upon meeting them, nor do I attempt to do it in everyday contact. For many reasons I limit any effort at thought perception to performances. A person's thoughts should be inviolate unless he wishes to divulge them. More than that, I'm not interested.

Thought perception in auditoriums, theaters or night clubs is obviously simpler, but more open to skepticism, than long-range thought reading where the subject cannot be seen but can be heard. Skepticism within the confines of a room results from the possibility of reading facial expressions or the possible use of stooges. Either way, the latter would be a risky undertaking.

I'd been fascinated with the possibilities of long-range mental telepathy since first reading of writer Harold Sherman's attempt to contact Sir Hubert Wilkins telepathically in the Arctic. The 1937 tests were believed to have failed until one night when Sherman couldn't concentrate because he saw flames. He did not know the location of the flames. Later it was revealed that at the same relative moment the explorer was too busy to "receive." He was helping to extinguish a fire. It could have been coincidence. The odds are much greater that it was not coincidence.

One of my first attempts at individual long-range thought perception was conducted on the *Mike Douglas Show* in October 1969. We decided to test this ESP concept as dramatically as possible, and in full audience view, over a 3,000-mile range. Mike was given a phone number by his staff and dialed it. Since the show was on tape, the person called would not be able to monitor it, see Douglas or myself. We were in the KYW-TV studio in Philadelphia.

The phone rang in Los Angeles and a female voice said "Hello." At first I didn't recognize the voice and neither did

Douglas. But soon Mike became aware that Carol Burnett was on the other end. She'd been informed that I would attempt to read her thoughts and that the only setting, in both places, would be a glass of water, a pad and a pencil.

Not at all certain it would work over this range of distance, I divided the test into three parts. First, I told her to look into the glass of water and think of any three- or four-digit number. In Philadelphia, I studied the surface of my water glass, hoping for the image of the numbers. (The water, acting as a mirror, was for my benefit, not hers.) In a moment I received the sequence and wrote it on a slate, which was immediately covered with masking tape so that Douglas could not see it. Additionally, I did not want to stand accused of altering figures before the end of the test.

I then asked her to think of a word, any word, and concentrate deeply on it. After a few seconds I received the word, seeing the image on the water, and wrote it on another slate, which was also quickly covered.

For the last step I said, "Carol, I don't know the room you're in, but look around it, think of some object in the room, anywhere in the room."

There was a pause, which should have told me something, but it didn't register. Then I heard her voice: "Yes, Kres, I'm thinking of something."

I received it and wrote it down.

Then Douglas pulled the first tape and Carol, from Los Angeles, repeated the three-digit number, 921. I'd hit and breathed a sigh of relief.

She called off the word, "baby," and the second tape was pulled. I'd gotten that one, too.

I asked, over the phone, what the object was, and she answered, "Well, I'm not at home, I'm in my agent's office and I'm looking at a painting on the wall. That's what I was thinking of."

The Douglas staff pulled the third tape and I'd written: *Bronze statue.*

Puzzled as well as disappointed, I admitted I'd made a

mistake. Yet I was certain that the image I'd received on the water surface—an image there but not there, mirrored from my mind—was a bronze statue.

Suddenly Carol yelped, one of those well-known, delightful Burnett yelps: "Kreskin, when you told me to think of something I changed my mind. The first thing I thought of was this bronze paperweight I'm holding. It's a small statue. But then I thought of the painting."

Now I understood the pause.

While I knew that short-range telepathy worked, within a room or building, or over a distance of a few miles within the city, I was now satisfied that it could travel thousands of miles between a "sender" and a "receiver" after telephonic rapport was established. It could deal in specifics if the contact was sharp. Carol Burnett, of course, was an excellent choice for the experiment. She was accustomed to concentration and receptive to the idea that it would work. Although we'd never met, we had seen each other on TV. The few minutes of conversation provided the required rapport. The test also convinced me, at last, that distance does not always decrease mental reception, unlike radio and video communication.

Even earlier than the Burnett test, groping on my own, I'd used a mass and rather scientific approach to long-range telepathy, acting as the "sender" rather than the "receiver." The concept was simple enough: I would sit in my office on West Fifty-seventh Street in New York for fourteen nights and concentrate on one subject each night, hopeful that X number of people could read my single thought. I was assuming some rapport might be possible on the basis that volunteers, though strangers, would have previously seen me and heard my voice on TV.

I decided on two hundred as a workable number but was astonished when thirty-eight hundred people, world-wide, volunteered for the test. They wrote in from Canada, England, Germany and Italy, as well as the United States. Representing a wide segment, fortunately, from show people to postmen, housewives and students, they included several astronauts and many professional categories. Three-quarters were women. There was no way of knowing whom to reject, so I accepted all of them. The test period was set between Sunday, March 17, and Saturday, March 30, 1968.

I instructed my secretary to select one hundred objects. Each item, placed in a sealed envelope, would be deposited in a shopping bag. There were no limitations except that the items would have to be small enough to be inserted into the envelopes. Some of her topics were found in newspapers. With her eyes closed, she put a knife randomly on dictionary pages and then copied the word that the blade hit. The scope, of course, was inexhaustible. Meanwhile we notified the volunteers that the test would run from 7 to 7:05, Eastern standard time, on each night, and that I would have no knowledge of the topic until I reached into the "grab bag" and ripped the envelope open. I would then sit at my desk for five minutes, thinking only of the object in my hand.

On the first night, Sunday, March 17, I reached for an envelope, opened it and extracted a Band-Aid. Wrapping it around my finger, I not only mentally identified the object, but gave a description of it. Attempting the deepest possible concentration, I repeated it over and over. I also attempted to "photograph" it in my mind and then send that picture in the manner that a wirephoto is sent.

Within two weeks after the first test, I discovered that I'd have to hire a staff to evaluate the results properly. Mail deluged the office as roughly ninety-five percent of the volunteers responded, not waiting until the completion of the fourteen nights.

The targets transmitted were:

1. March 17—Band-Aid.
2. March 18—Newspaper clipping of actress Elizabeth Taylor, who had flown into New York from Europe. She was dressed in white fur, holding a black pocketbook, standing near the aircraft.

3. March 19—Garter strap and button, in white cloth.
4. March 20—Lock of hair.
5. March 21—Cotton swab, stick with cotton on both ends.
6. March 22—"Press Only" badge.
7. March 23—News-clip photo of oceanographic lab.
8. March 24—Woman's beige-and-white leather belt.
9. March 25—Magazine cutout of portrait of Picasso's son.
10. March 26—Red golf tee.
11. March 27—Cutout of Miller High Life beer ad.
12. March 28—(A) News clip of prisoner in yard after prison riot. (B) Silver bottle top from nonfat milk.
13. March 29—I slept during testing period, hopeful of drawing a blank.
14. March 30—Ad clip of woman brushing teeth while holding an aspirin for a headache.

Two hundred of the "receivers" had almost direct hits on each night. Twenty-five had three or more hits; seventy-five had two hits. Over one hundred had one correct hit. Five percent of all participants had significant or "near misses." Although these percentages might seem small in relation to the roughly three thousand participants, I think they are remarkable. I would have been pleased with fifty direct hits.

We found that the largest percentage of success with a single target was the news picture of Elizabeth Taylor, dressed in white ermine, holding a white pocketbook and a white muff. Oddly enough, no one named her. However, a number said they "saw a picture of a famous actress or a famous lady." Several said she was "dressed in total white standing by an airplane." This was almost the identical description I was trying to send that night. I did name her, hopeful that a few people would receive it. Apparently it is much more difficult to "receive" a name than to receive a mental picture.

On March 20, many people thought of a "pine tree" when the target was a "lock of hair." There is a symbolic similarity— a topping or spread of material. On March 26, a number of returns named the Eiffel Tower. In analyzing this impression (though I may be reaching), I feel it worth noting that the Eiffel Tower does resemble an inverted golf tee, the target for that evening's test. A small percentage sent various and confused images the night that I slept.

A total of twenty-eight cities in the United States and Canada were involved in the test, and five European cities. Philadelphia had the highest overall score. Washington, D.C., had no success at all. I have no idea how to evaluate these results aside from the obvious fact that there were more "sensitive" volunteers in the City of Brotherly Love than in the city of politics.

It was the first such test, to my knowledge, on a national and international scale, and I think it was successful. Six months was required to correlate the percentages. Among other indications, we found that women scored higher than men. This doesn't necessarily indicate that women are more sensitive to ESP. More tests would have to be made with equal proportions of male and female subjects. However, I've generally found that females are inclined to be less openly skeptical of ESP. Males may not express their opinions to the same degree.

The next great adventure in this area is outer-space telepathy. Astronaut Edgar Mitchell attempted to make that bridge during the moon shot of Apollo 14, January and February 1971. Unfortunately there wasn't enough time for careful preparation, and Mitchell's other duties understandably prevented anything more than a sketchy test. He "sent" twice on the outward flight and made another two attempts on the return. The results were disappointing. Even so, Mitchell opened the door to new American experiments in ESP.

Once more, Russia is ahead of the United States in this area, having already experimented for a number of years. Advances have been claimed. Outer-space ESP has been attempted, and they've gone in the other direction, placing a "receiver" four stories beneath the earth with the "sender" on the surface attempting to control thinking, response and behavior.

For a nation that has not permitted public discussion of even psychoanalysis and that has cast Dr. Freud as a dangerous influence, it is both interesting and somewhat frightening to observe the Soviet Union's current insatiable efforts in parapsychology and related fields.

In researching their book on current efforts in Russia, Sheila Ostrander and Lynn Schroeder noted an emphasis on the "sender" rather than the "receiver," which is the reverse of the American interest. The Russians, they told me, appear to be looking for people who can project ideas into the minds of others. They are also apparently showing a great deal of interest in psychokinesis.

When the authors appeared on my program, I showed their Russian film clips of a woman who sat at a table "causing" buttons, matchsticks and other objects to move by mental force. Her hands were at least a foot from the objects, her feet visible and motionless under the table. She also moved, on camera, a compass dial by holding her hands over it. Prior to this sequence, she was examined to make certain that no tiny magnets had been hidden beneath the fingernails. Evaluation of film is always difficult, but this footage was totally unconvincing. I do not doubt that natural and physical magnetism can move a compass dial under certain circumstances. However, the Russian footage looked and "felt" staged.

The authors said that the Russian scientists they interviewed repeatedly beseeched them to tell their American colleagues to use ESP only for peaceful purposes. Much as I'd prefer to think otherwise, I'm strongly of the opinion that the Soviets doth protest too much.

Not surprisingly, Josef Stalin banned all research into ESP. Yet, surreptitiously, long ago, he used Wolf Messing, the famous Russian mentalist, as a consultant. Stalin obviously believed in the scientific applications of parapsychology, but his own devious mentality saw fit to save it for future machinations.

Messing had fled from the Nazi invasion of Poland after Hitler put a price tag of two hundred thousand Deutsche marks on his head. His reputation was such that when he reached Russia, Stalin wanted proof of his ability. He reportedly told Messing to rob the Bank of Moscow of one hundred thousand rubles, using his power of suggestion or "hypnosis," or whatever he wanted to term the talent. Accordingly, Messing wrote a note on school scratch paper and visited the bank. Approaching a cashier, he took the note from his attaché case and passed it over the counter. Messing also claims to have "willed" the cashier to disburse the money. However it was done, Messing went back to the Kremlin, mission accomplished, along with a few of Stalin's officials who had witnessed the "robbery." He then returned the package of rubles to the cashier, who promptly suffered a heart attack. The story, true or not, added to the legend of the great Wolf Messing, who is still alive, still entertaining, at last report.

To the general world at least, the parapsychology efforts in Russia surfaced in a benign way in the sixties when it became clear that her Olympic weight lifters and gymnasts had been trained in autosuggestion. Both of these endeavors, basically involving individual prowess, are excellent platforms for improvement by autosuggestion. Now the prospect is that Russia may be leading the world in a field potentially more important than the Olympics.

In 1960 the late Dr. Leonid Vasiliev, one of the Soviet Union's foremost parapsychologists, established a special laboratory for telepathy research at the University of Leningrad. That same year Dr. Vasiliev startled a distinguished group of Russian scientists by blithely discussing "mental radio." ESP was coming out from under Red Square wraps.

In 1962 Dr. Vasiliev was finally permitted to publish his book *Experiments in Mental Suggestion*, detailing work that dated back to 1932. Sometime during the early thirties, about the time that Dr. Rhine began his work at Duke, Vasiliev, then at the St. Petersburg Brain Institute, was "given orders to find a solution to telepathy." The belief was that a physical explanation to telepathy existed, and an attempt would be made to take it out of the supernormal. Remaining in that foggy area, it posed a threat to dialectic materialism. If the Russians have indeed found a "solution to telepathy," which is doubtful, they haven't shared it. But another step in the early sixties was the founding of a Commission for the Study of Mental Suggestion at the St. Petersburg Brain Institute.

A considerable time before his death, Dr. Vasiliev said, "Discovery of the energy held in the ESP phenomena will be comparable to the discovery of atomic energy."

[11]

My reasoning factors often become my enemies.

If I begin to evaluate a situation critically, apply logic and reason to it, I find I'm in danger of destroying what information I'm receiving from my subject, or my guides. The information, or image, must come impulsively and spontaneously. It must be accepted in that manner and not examined.

In Indianapolis, I was trying to find an object hidden somewhere within a twenty-five-story building. My guides, Governor Edgar D. Whitcomb and two high city officials, were by my side constantly—thinking only of where they'd hidden the paper decal. To avoid suspicion I request more than one guide, hoping for three or four well-known people. Thus, a "telepathy" committee is usually formed.

For thirty-five minutes, in this case, I was completely stymied. I was almost on the verge of nervous exhaustion, ready to quit. It was all the more embarrassing, since United Press International and a local TV crew were covering the test.

I kept saying to Governor Whitcomb's committee, "For God's sake, tell me mentally what floor it's on." The signals I was getting were ridiculous, or so I thought.

I got off the elevator on floor after floor. Nothing on the third, nothing on the fourth, zero on the eighth. Finally, we reached the twenty-fourth floor, then the twenty-fifth. I was soaked with perspiration.

Then I realized what had happened. Once again, through trying to reason, I'd become my own archenemy. I had set up a mental barrier which made it impossible for me to perceive their thoughts. I had kept saying to them, insisting, "Think of what floor it is on." I'd become more angry with each moment.

Maybe it wasn't on any floor!

I raced back into the elevator and there was the paper decal, cleverly hidden behind the inspection sign on the elevator wall.

For another similar test in the same city, a sheriff handed me a cigarette lighter. I was to locate the owner, one of six hundred thousand inhabitants within city limits. Climbing into a limousine, I began the search while the sheriff concentrated on the location of the owner. I was permitted to talk to the driver, directing him from thoughts received from the law officer.

At one point I stopped the car and got out, the sheriff and TV crew following. Receiving distinct, positive information, I walked about a mile, finally turning into a bank. When I approached an elderly teller he gave me such a blank, almost hostile look that my reasoning told me I was wrong.

Positive now that the owner of the lighter was in the bank, I studied other employees, even customers, but was drawn back to the teller each time as the sheriff, whom I could not see, kept mentally insisting that I'd found the right man. It was the simple "hot" and "cold" of the childhood game "Huckle Buckle Beanstalk."

Finally I went up. "Sir," I said, "either this is yours or I've blown the test."

It seemed an eternity until the teller broke into a smile. "It's mine."

To locate him had taken forty-eight minutes. At least twenty minutes, including the one-mile walk, could have been cut had I accepted, without question or reasoning, the sheriff's explicit directions to the bank and his unequivocal mental commands toward the hostile-looking teller.

As part of each concert, to combat skepticism and the accusation that my subjects are paid confederates, I request that my pay check be hidden. I make the claim that I'll find it or the sponsors will have the benefit of a free performance, so I do have an incentive to find it.

To date, among other odd places, my check has been stuffed into a turkey at the Waldorf-Astoria Hotel; nestled in a brassiere; frozen in an ice tray; taped to a board ripped up from the stage and replaced; tucked beneath a man's upper plate in an audience of eight thousand at Northwestern University.

The hiding and guiding committees resort to deviousness beyond belief. College students can think of hiding places that would defeat the FBI. They defy all logic and produce migraines. I ask for it. But it is, after all, hard-earned money and I prefer to find it.

Once, in a Methodist church in Caldwell, I suddenly stopped in an aisle and blurted out, "Gun," seeming to be drawn toward a man sitting a few spaces over in one pew. I requested that he take off his coat and then saw the gun in a shoulder holster. He was a plain-clothes detective, I later learned. The check was in an empty bullet chamber, rolled to pencil size.

Private parties, which I do occasionally, often give birth to particularly elaborate hiding schemes. The hosts have weeks to think about secreting the fee. At one, in Rieglesville, Pennsylvania, I kept going back into the library and pulling out an expensive leather-bound book, thumbing through it and putting it back. The check was in that specific book according to the mental message I was getting from my hostess. Finally I understood that she wanted me to rip the binding of the book, an act completely against my nature. However, I obeyed the thought and out peeked the check. She'd gone to the trouble of having a shoemaker open the binding, insert the check and then carefully restitch the spine.

Depending on the situation, size and nature of the group, and the length of the performance, I occasionally challenge the committee to provide a thought-perception *action* test, any sequence of three or four physical actions, prior to the "hidden check" routine. Logically, the test will key the finding of the check. Wolf Messing has been using similar action sequences for some years.

In one such test I remember a sudden urge to remove a pack of cards from the stage table. I thumbed through them, following the mental directions. I found myself holding the ace of spades and dropping the balance of the deck to the floor. I awaited the next signal and tore the ace of spades in half. It did not seem sufficient, so I tore each piece again. I was as mystified as the audience when a third signal told me to toss one of the pieces in front of me, turn, toss another, turn again, toss another. A final turn and toss.

The committee chairman then stepped up to inform me I was ready to proceed with the check finding. I'd passed the test of tossing the four corners of the ace of spades north, east, south and west. My check would be in a westerly direction.

ESP action tests tend to be difficult simply because of the almost endless possibilities within any given room or group of people. I can't recall that any two tests have been of the same nature.

David McCallum, the Scottish actor, one of the stars of TV's *Man From U.N.C.L.E.,* went backstage on my TV show to prepare such a test. Assisted by three audience members, he wrote out three action steps and placed them in separate envelopes. Returning to the stage area, one committee member began concentrating on the first test.

Soon I found myself walking up to different men in the audience in response to the concentration. It took me a moment to realize that the signal had something to do with ties. There was a negative whenever I stopped in front of a tieless man. Or there was no signal. Finally I understood that I was to take a tie off. I accomplished that and waited.

McCallum then opened the other two envelopes and began to concentrate. I found myself moving along the front row and then stop by a woman. It did not make sense (the tests are seldom very logical) but I laced the tie around her ankle and secured it. My final direction seemed to be a request to bring the lady to the stage. I complied.

The three actions matched the committee's slips of paper. More than any other ESP experiment, the action tests indicate the need to carry out the perceived thought without evaluation. This is particularly true in seeking the location of the performance fee.

People sometimes ask, "When you come into the auditorium to find the check, what is going on inside you? On the conscious level, do you try to do anything you can analyze and explain later? Does a picture of the hiding place flash through your mind? What really happens?"

This advanced form of "Huckle Buckle Beanstalk" requires, once again, that I detach myself from the immediate environment, concentrating only on the thoughts and directions of my guides, who are also the "hiders." I even lose them as people, not aware if they are male or female. I concentrate on reading every direction, every clue, and sensitize myself to hear or see any supportive factors beyond the perceived thought. In this experiment, I've found, the guide is desperately trying to penetrate. It can be likened to a highly stimulated game of charades when the leader is practically standing on his ear to get his point across. It is much easier, for me, when one or two guides function, as in the McCallum test. A whole committee tends to fill the communication with confusion.

So far, in thousands of attempts, I've only failed once.

During an early-evening performance in the East, I had about twenty people sitting in a semicircle facing the audience. I was beginning a demonstration in suggestibility. My glasses were off and I was bending over a woman, standing behind her, talking to the audience. She raised her arm to fix her hair and accidentally hit my hand, jabbing the stem of my glasses into my left eye. I thought the blindness was momentary until someone yelled. Blood was streaming down my cheek.

After the performance was canceled, a doctor's quick examination revealed no permanent damage. It would heal within a week or so. I went on to New York that night because I had an engagement at an all-night private Park Avenue party. I managed to fumble through the ESP and suggestibility phases and began the search for my check at about 5 A.M. but soon forfeited. The eye was throbbing; I was now loaded with painkillers and couldn't concentrate.

A reporter once said, "That's an exciting game, isn't it? Playing hide-and-go-seek with your own money."

All I could think of was "Yes."

[12]

I suppose that anyone who calls himself a mentalist invites participation in strange affairs. Occasionally, wherever I am, the phone will ring and I find myself involved in a matter completely unrelated to show business. Some are interesting; others I prefer to duck. There are also those in which I can be of no help.

A few times I've been requested to assist in locating missing persons by thought perception. As much as I'd like to help, I have to decline. I don't think it is possible unless the person who is lost is "sending" a call for help, and is also wise enough to pinpoint the location and have a sensitive "receiver" tuning in. A perceptive parent would be more likely to receive such information by telepathy than any expert. The idea of a psychic locating a lost child in the wilderness is fine for fiction but mostly pathetic in a real situation. However, there are mental techniques which can work in other cases.

Shortly after the Sharon Tate murders in 1969 in California's exclusive Bel-Air section, the infamous Charles Manson "family" case, I received a phone call from Robert Houghton, chief of detectives of the Los Angeles police department. In the hours immediately following the grisly deaths, it appeared that some type of cult might have been involved. At least, the slayings looked to be ritualistic, so the police had begun probing into all cult possibilities, hoping to develop leads. One logical avenue was to ask the aid of occultists. Several psychics and mediums talked to Houghton and gave him certain judgments.

I explained that I was not a psychic but would be willing to listen and talk and make any contribution I could. Houghton told me what the Hollywood psychics had said. It was pretty flimsy and speculative, in my opinion. Later their reasoning, from the occult point of view, was proven completely wrong.

Then, as now, my only possible contribution would have been to work with a witness, someone who had actually seen the crime take place but could not recall certain details due to trauma, or someone who had seen the participants leaving the scene but could not describe the persons or the automobile because of trauma. My role would have been to attempt to draw out information or clarify it, using modifications of the same techniques I use onstage.

In fact, major law-enforcement agencies could well use at least one expert interrogator trained in techniques to stimulate recall. It might save time and money, and possibly contribute to justice.

As a minor example, while appearing in Dallas I received a request from a friend, a lawyer, with a wealthy but slightly eccentric and bothersome lady client whose household staff, the butler and the maid, was under suspicion of jewelry theft. Two very expensive earrings and a bracelet were missing but had not been reported to the police because of a tax situation. I pointed out that I couldn't work with anyone unless he cooperated, and that if the butler or the maid was guilty they wouldn't lend themselves to incrimination. I might detect a lie if I talked to them but preferred not to because I could be wrong. However, I agreed to visit the client.

We went back over the night, a very muddled period, during which the jewelry had disappeared. The lady had been drinking heavily at a party. She finally remembered taking off the earrings and bracelet after coming home. Piecing together every move that she could recall, we finally located the jewelry behind a vanity in her dressing room. I think she wanted to blame her staff instead of too many Scotch-and-sodas.

Another case involved personal injury. An insurance company was refusing to pay a claim after an accident near Montclair, New Jersey, maintaining driver negligence. The lady was not able to recall exactly what had happened before her car went out of control. We had three or four sessions to work back to the moment of the crash, finally pinning down a pile of wet leaves on a curve as the point of loss of control. In previous testimony she had not mentioned the leaves, and other skid marks had confused the path of the car on the slick surface.

Perhaps the most interesting consultation came out of an FBI request after a bank robbery in Passaic, New Jersey. A witness had been in front of the bank during the getaway. She had seen the robbers, the car and probably the license plate, but could give no descriptions. Naturally, she'd been terrified at the time. The FBI brought her to my office.

After talking to her for a few minutes I turned off most of the lights. I had her gaze at the darkened wall, and then asked her to picture some simple objects. As she relaxed and began to accept the fact that she might be able to recall much more of the scene, I had her reconstruct the getaway moments. Soon she began to add movement and sound to her descriptions, which she had failed to do under her previous taped questioning. At that point I felt that her imagination had been triggered. She then added a few other details and was finally able to "see" the car and describe it, but not the license plate.

"You've been to comedy movies where the film is backed up, haven't you?" I remember saying. "Everything comes forward to you on the screen."

"Yes."

"Okay, keep looking at the wall and back that car up."

When it came close enough in her mental re-creation of the scene, she did "read off" the license number, very precisely, and it assisted the FBI in breaking the case.

There was no psychic phenomenon swirling here. The trauma of that afternoon had blocked her unconscious. She had temporarily rejected both the car and the license plate. All she needed was a guide back to the circumstances.

[13]

A strong belief in ESP appears to be a major factor in its everyday use. The nonbeliever is likely to shrug off even a decisive feeling. He simply cannot accept the idea that he has received a compelling mental direction.

At four o'clock on Sunday afternoon, November 12, 1972, one very strong believer, Mrs. Leticia Shindo, of Scottsdale, Arizona, was suddenly struck with the possibility that an ailing friend, Jim Grover, who lived sixty miles away, was in trouble. He did not have a telephone.

"I had a premonition," she said later. "I had vibrations around myself. I think in my mind that Mr. Grover needs help."

A few minutes later she told her sixteen-year-old son, George, of the premonition. "That's funny," he replied. "I just had the same feeling about Mr. Grover." The fifty-eight-year-old bachelor lived in a desolate area near Florence, site of the Arizona State Prison.

Responding to the premonition, not questioning it, Mrs. Shindo and George, accompanied by his seventeen-year-old friend, drove to Grover's small house, reaching it just before six o'clock. They found that the front door was locked, a measure seldom taken by Grover. Few people ever came near the house. Using an emergency key that Grover had given her, Mrs. Shindo opened the door and they went in cautiously. Seconds later a tall man holding a gun stepped into the front room.

"What's happened to Mr. Grover?" Mrs. Shindo asked.

"Nothing, lady, nothing," the man answered.

But Mrs. Shindo's "premonition" had not been false. When she looked into the kitchen she saw the ill, fatigued Grover sitting in a chair, held captive by another man, later identified as Charles Schmid, the infamous "Pied Piper of Tucson." Both men were convicted murderers and had escaped the previous day from the nearby state prison. Schmid had brutally killed three children, and Raymond Hudgens had been convicted of killing his estranged wife and her parents. A massive manhunt, stretching into California, was under way.

Offering herself and the boys as additional hostages, Mrs. Shindo agreed to drive the killers to Tempe, Arizona, where they were finally captured. None of the hostages was harmed.

There is little doubt that mental communication was established that day between Grover, also a strong believer in ESP, and Mrs. Shindo. He was "sending" a call for help.

It is quite likely that hundreds, if not thousands, of communications similar to those established between Mrs. Shindo and Grover take place daily. Few ever involve escaped killers and consequently are not reported. Those involving death, accidental or natural, are seldom revealed unless the key persons are prominent or the circumstances unusual.

But scientific evidence of two-way telepathic communication is mounting as researchers bank experiences related by the general public. It does not appear to be as common as the spontaneous one-way flashes, but there is indication that it could be developed, particularly among close friends or loved ones.

Rolland Smith, now a CBS-TV news commentator in New York, told me of a dangerous flight that he made in Vietnam during a time when his wife, back in Indiana, was expecting a baby. On takeoff he had discovered that the military plane was loaded with ammunition. They were flying over an area held by the Vietcong, known to be heavily fortified with antiaircraft guns and rockets. Smith said he'd never before prayed so hard. Suddenly he had a vision of his wife giving birth and asked his cameraman to note the time.

A week later, arriving safely back in Indianapolis, he started to tell his wife of the vision, but she interrupted to say that she had seen him in an aircraft, experiencing great fear, at about the same moment the baby was born. A check revealed that the times coincided almost to the minute recorded by the hospital as the time of birth.

Several summers ago I awakened from a troubled night's sleep to face a day which included a flight. I was booked to open that evening in a hotel at Lake Placid, New York. I blamed the restless night on high heat, and also blamed heat for my negative mood. I couldn't get myself together. I wasted time, delayed packing, and finally had to apologize to my family for being churlish. I was terribly depressed but didn't know why, aside from the humidity.

Going to the airport, I detoured through Newark instead of my usual fast route via the Garden State Parkway. I had no reason to do it and soon found myself tied up in city traffic. What should have been a quick, easy freeway drive to Newark Airport had turned into stop-and-go. By the time I'd cleared the midtown clutter it was nearing ten o'clock, flight time, and I broke speed limits all the way to the parking lot.

Checking in, nerves shot, soaked to the skin, I was told by the girl at the desk "to run for it." But by the time I got to the gate, the aircraft door was closed and the plane was beginning to taxi. I walked back to the desk and the same girl arranged for me to take a helicopter to La Guardia and then catch another plane.

I inquired about my luggage. It didn't seem to be around. The girl answered vaguely, "Oh, yes," but appeared to do nothing. I blamed it on the ninety-degree heat. She'd already tagged it, wherever it was, and I assumed it had gone on to Lake Placid.

When I landed at Lake Placid after a rough flight from La Guardia, I suddenly became obsessed with my missing luggage. I watched as the old-fashioned cart emptied the aircraft, but I couldn't spot my bags. The small Lake Placid airport promised to check with Newark and send out a tracer.

In the afternoon I shopped in the village for a dark suit, shirt and tie, hopeful that by morning the airline would find the missing bags. Twenty minutes before I went onstage that night, the airline called to inform me that my bags had been shifted in Albany to the original flight from Newark. Well, when would they arrive? My annoyance ceased when the voice informed me that the original flight had crashed en route to Lake Placid in a cow pasture. I hadn't been listening to the radio.

In trying to analyze this as premonition, I went back to the sleepless night, to the depressed mood, to procrastination in packing, to taking a detour that I had never taken before, to missing the plane by less than sixty seconds, finally to the look of complete detachment on the face of the girl at the airline desk. Or I "read it" that way. Perhaps they were all signposts, with the Newark detour as the crucial indicator.

From such incidents, and many others that are in my files, I'm convinced that the unconscious mind is as sensitive, and on some occasions more sensitive, than the conscious mind. In telepathic situations, it obviously has a longer range. In apparent incidents of premonition, it often defies any current understanding.

I'm also fully convinced that if we all sensitized our minds, developed the natural powers that are there, we could avoid many hazards. There is every reason to believe that we do have a "radar" that we seldom turn on. And premonition seems to be a definite part of ESP.

About 1850, Mark Twain dreamed of seeing his brother Henry lying in a metal coffin, dressed in one of Twain's own suits, holding a bouquet of flowers in his hands. The center flower was a red rose. The coffin rested between two chairs.

Two days after this dream a boat exploded on the Mississippi and Henry Clemens was killed. Hurrying home, Twain found his brother lying in a metal casket, dressed in a suit he owned, clasping a bouquet of flowers. The center flower was a red rose. Had Twain arrived a few minutes later the coffin would have been placed between two chairs. They had already been drawn up.

Similar incidents may have happened to any number of John Does but would never have reached public print.

Harry Kellar, like most magicians, was a die-hard skeptic where psychic phenomena were concerned. Yet when he came face to face with premonition, he was as vulnerable as any nonprofessional. Staying overnight with a friend, he awoke to find the man depressed and troubled. Over breakfast, the friend confided that he'd had a dream. He'd seen a devastating train wreck; many people had been killed. Kellar was scheduled to depart that afternoon by rail. The magician thought about it for a while and then submitted to the dream premonition. He postponed his trip for twenty-four hours. Lucky that he did. The friend's dream came true that evening.

There is definite indication that people are capable of receiving telepathic messages while asleep, possibly even while dreaming. Occupied with the dream, the mind may not be too receptive to outside interruptions. But it is another of the unknowns, and a strong signal could possibly break through the dream. Being physical as well as psychical, the brain does appear to rest but it is doubtful that it is totally asleep. It remains partially active, receptive to messages from within a room or house: an unusual noise, a baby's cry, a creaking door, thunder. Or on occasion, perhaps, messages from a distance, long or short.

Arthur Godfrey tells of an incident that occurred when he was in the Coast Guard. One night at sea he thought he awakened and saw his father floating away from him. Or perhaps, he said, within the distortion of his mind, he was still asleep. He thought, however, that his eyes were open at the time he had the vision. (That, too, is possible. We can dream with our eyes open.) In the morning Godfrey received a message that his father had passed away. He radioed back and requested the exact time of his father's death. It matched, within a few minutes, the time that Godfrey had noted as the apparent wake-up time.

A few years ago a reporter for the Newark *Star-Ledger* related a somewhat similar case that took place in Elizabeth, New Jersey. A wire story had been filed from Europe with the scant detail that a young serviceman, taking a flight from Germany to surprise his parents, had been killed when the plane crashed on takeoff. Thinking that the Army had already notified next of kin, the reporter went to the house and found the mother in hysterics. She said, "You don't need to tell me." She'd awakened a few hours earlier and had seen her son in flames. The Army did not get around to notification until the next day.

Reported daily, weekly, such incidents are common and add solid foundation to the need for extensive research in sleep and dream telepathy. Such study has recently been carried out at the Maimonides Medical Center's Dream Laboratory in Brooklyn, New York, under the direction of Dr. Stanley Krippner. It was long overdue and has provided much added knowledge to the simple human experience of dreaming.

Visually, as well as with sensors, Dr. Krippner has observed sleeping subjects while they were in the dream state. By attaching the electroencephalogram (EEG) and other sensitive instruments, Krippner has been able to study nervous activity, including the REM factor—rapid eye movement—which is the first indication of the dream state. The eyes move and react normally, even though the subject is asleep. If the imagination sends a car toward the dreaming subject, the pupils will expand; they will contract if an object recedes into the distance. If the subject is dreaming with eyes open, bright light will cause the iris to close; dim light will open it.

In telepathic experiments, Krippner found that sometimes he could have an awake "sender," sitting nearby the sleeping subject, establish communication. He would hand the sender an envelope which contained an emotionally dynamic topic, usually a newsprint photo. As an example, I remember that he used one from the John Kennedy funeral. The sender then concentrated on the scene, attempting to project his thoughts —the mind picture—to the hopefully receptive sleeper. When the dream state began, the message was continued. After a while the subject was awakened and asked to describe the dream.

In some cases, particularly when a message as dramatic as the Kennedy funeral was used, the subjects "incorporated" the picture into the dream or dreams. *The only possible source was the sender seated nearby.*

One significance of Dr. Krippner's exceptional work is an indication that our minds have the capability of receiving information and temporarily storing it while the body is dormant. In attempting to sort it all out, it is difficult to distinguish the shadings of difference between telepathy, premonition and even clairvoyance, with the subject awake or asleep. They all seem to be under the same general dome, but there is overlapping which compounds the simple truth that the entire phenomenon is basically unexplained. This leads to wide distrust if not disbelief in all the manifestations.

However, for every notable skeptic, past and present, there have been notable believers. Mark Twain coined the term "mental telegraphy" when his letters crossed letters from friends in which they discussed topics he'd already covered in his. None other than Albert Einstein wrote the introduction for the German edition of Upton Sinclair's *Mental Radio*. The subject was telepathy.

The ever conservative American Association for the Advancement of Science did not welcome ESP until 1971 when it finally accepted the subject as a legitimate area for scientific research, but its approval, primarily engineered by the anthropologist Dr. Margaret Mead, was a major breakthrough. Those involved in serious research were at last encouraged and awarded some respect. In a measure Dr. Rhine, scoffed at for a quarter of a century, was finally vindicated.

[14]

Déjà vu, the French term for the illusion of having encountered something before when it is actually being experienced for the first time, is another of those psychical mysteries that has been around for centuries and is still not resolved. It has happened to everyone: you walk into a room and get a feeling that you have been in it before; you have a conversation and there is a strange familiarity about it as if the words have already been said with someone else; you meet a person and have the strange feeling you've met him before, but know you can't have.

Among other claims, déjà vu has been used in support of reincarnation and again gained momentary credence when "Bridey Murphy" bobbed up in the mid-fifties, following the same path of similar reincarnated ladies and gentlemen in the early part of the century. Without reincarnation to confuse the subject, déjà vu is apparently a natural phenomenon. It is sometimes lumped with the occult because it is not understood. Wherever its home should be, it is not in ESP.

One theory is that upon entering a room, a person sees X number of details, the brain recording them instantly though unconsciously. A moment later he sees them conciously, becoming fully aware of them, and feels a strange familiarity about them, even the possibility that he has seen them before.

That theory doesn't quite work for me. The average person well knows what he has seen several seconds before. As time goes on, he will see more but not usually in a frame of familiarity as if he had been in the room previously. He will normally see the room exactly as it is.

The theory of déjà vu that I tend to accept involves "unconscious memories." A room is entered and the eyes go to a crack in the wall, or a couch is in a position similar to one of past experience. Perhaps the color is the same or close. Sunlight might have faded it, similar to one from past experience. It does not bring back an entire experience but there is enough of it to churn dormant memories.

If it was a positive example, a room from childhood re-entered, not an illusion, why not absolute recognition? Why only a vague familiarity? Most déjà-vu experiences are vague and blurred.

Déjà vu appears to be somewhat in the same psychic-phenomenon area as glossolalia, or speaking in foreign tongues. Some religious cults practice a form of it, claiming that it is "talk with God," but the words that flow out seem more gibberish than language. I've taped them and remain bewildered by them.

However, there are investigated, recorded cases where a person, years into life, suddenly began speaking fluent Latin, Greek or other languages. The mystery of one lady who unexplainably began spouting Greek was traced to childhood, the usual origin. Her mother was a cleaner in a Greek Orthodox church and rectory. The child was often around when the priests conversed or said prayers aloud. Under a traumatic condition in late life she went "back" to the rectory, again churning dormant memories.

Memories of dramatic incidents can be brought back, when the subject is wide awake or in a so-called trance. If the imagination is sufficiently stimulated, and an association is established, the patient may remember details and even act some of them out. But he is not "regressed" in the absolute sense of the word.

Some doctors still believe there is a therapeutic value in the regression process. However, research by Dr. T. X. Barber, of the Medfield Institute, Boston, and others, indicates that when a person is "sent back" to a particular day, or a part of his life, he'll do an excellent job of inventing what can't be remembered. Incidents developed by regression were researched. Some were partially true; others were complete fabrication.

And "Bridey Murphy" was among the better fabrications of this century. With amateur hypnotist Morey Bernstein as her guide, Ruth Simmons, or Virginia Ty, not only went back to the age of three months in this lifetime but then tunneled centuries into another. She danced jigs, reportedly, and talked in an Irish brogue, all to the ecstasy of the reincarnationists. Then *Life* magazine exposed that as a child she had lived in an Irish neighborhood in Chicago. With or without that exposure, for what it meant, Bridey didn't go into enough detail of her previous life to substantiate the slightest possibility that she'd ever existed in the land of leprechauns.

Meanwhile Mr. Bernstein made a modest sum from his best seller and the subsequent Paramount motion picture, which took even more liberties. The subject of reincarnation remains irresistible to a portion of the public, and Bridey will no doubt return under other names.

Beating Bridey to the literary punch was "Patience Worth," other-world entity for a Mrs. Florence Lenore Curran, in 1913. Patience, it was claimed, was an English girl who had lived during the reign of Queen Elizabeth I, and through the automatic writing of Mrs. Curran turned out several books and some poetry. Purists will say that this is not really a case of reincarnation, but I don't know where else to put it.

The credo of the Theosophical Society, founded in 1875, is based on reincarnation. H. G. Wells mechanized the whole interesting process in his book *The Time Machine*, published in 1901.

Actually, the old poltergeist, a first-rate entertainer, is of much more amusement than any reincarnated folk. The German word means "noisy ghost," and he has a colorful, active juvenile history. A silent ghost is of no use to anyone. Without footsteps or rapping, hurling objects about, he is rather a waste. Being invisible, supposedly, the only way he can attract attention, like a spoiled child, is to make a nuisance of himself. So the poltergeist, in his most material form, slams doors, throws plates across the room and in general raises Cain.

There is one constant about the mischievous poltergeist: he rarely seems to haunt a house unless children are present. In his *Haunted Houses*, author Hereward Carrington noted that most "poltergeisted dwellings" had at least one child in the pre-teen or early-teen stage.

Of course there are barns and abandoned houses and old factories and moors and glens and mountains, bridges, too, said to be inhabited by ghosts, but these seem to be a different species, if one accepts their existence. Notably, they are not violent. Perhaps they are weary ghosts.

One of the more recent spectacular American poltergeist inhabitations took place in the James H. Hermann home on Long Island, in New York. The quiet, conservative Catholic family was being disturbed by violent noises and tossed objects. It was a typical example of the German wraith, first recorded at Bingen-am-Rhein in A.D. 355, last appearing in Bremen in 1965, and in Rosenheim in Bavaria in 1967.

A few scientists and psychic investigators, including the very knowledgeable Dr. J. G. Pratt, formerly on Dr. Rhine's staff at Duke, visited the house. While Pratt was there, a door opened and a globe flew across the room. In a month's time, Pratt noted sixty-seven unexplained incidents. Several magicians, experts at making things "fly," requested permission to visit the house but the family preferred to remain "quiet," though they hosted Edward R. Murrow for *Person to Person* and *Life* magazine.

The Long Island inhabitation did not break the tradition. The Hermann's teen-age son, James, was present, somewhere in the house, each time the poltergeist performed.

As usual, the scientists and psychics came up with the same theories: (1) The house was occupied by a ghost or spirit that was never laid to rest because of a dramatic incident involving his death. Unsettled, unwanted, he demonstrated with hyperactivity. (2) The teen-ager was releasing an energy force, RSPK, or "recurrent spontaneous psychokinesis," which caused the disturbances. (3) The adolescent was having a marvelous time with his prankish tricks.

I'm usually inclined to accept No. 3, but acknowledge the possibility of psychokinesis being involved with the teen-ager unaware of his actions. To the relief of everyone, the poltergeist seems to depart when public attention subsides and the teen-ager grows up.

[15]

Some parapsychologists are concerned about the current popularity and even commercialization of ESP, of which I'm certainly guilty, but I think it is generally healthy, reflecting public interest. Such interest may be transformed into support for further research and development. Popular writing on the subject, though it is seldom qualified as speculation, does not necessarily do lasting damage except to the egos of a self-appointed few in academe.

Aside from my own show, which is entertainment-demonstration-participation, television has made a few other stabs at ESP. *The Sixth Sense*, a dramatic series, was canceled because of low ratings. It was not very realistic and I suspect the writers never took time to really explore the field for dramatic possibilities, or the producers had a preconceived notion of what ESP was all about, entangling it with the occult. Much earlier, Vincent Price emceed a short-lived show with pretested subjects doing Rhine-type demonstrations.

Until the day we measurably expand our knowledge of extrasensory perception, we should utilize what little is known of it, using it without fear and without attaching mysticism to the phenomenon. For this reason, mainly, in the early seventies I put together two games involving ESP principles. They're simple enough for children to play, yet are designed to satisfy adult complexities.

I can already hear the gasps of conservative psychologists, but I think it is healthy to approach the subject, at this point, as a game to be played and solved, slicing away as much of the scientific jargon as possible, invading the areas staked out, claimed and inflated by a tiny group of theorists who seem to be motivated as much by self-preservation as by research goals.

Why should the natural workings of the human mind be discussed in hushed tones or described in terms that few of us can spell, much less understand? Why not use games to explore possibilities?

I had a hunch that the public might react favorably to "mind" games. Then Lou Reda, who is not above being brash at times, went to Max Hess, owner of the Hess Department Store in Allentown. He asked Max to introduce the "ESP" game. Hess agreed but was startled when Reda said that the debut should take place in New York rather than in Allentown. Hess eventually sponsored it at the Americana Hotel in New York, drawing more than a hundred press members. Over two million copies were sold in less than a year. The public was obviously interested.

Whatever the feelings of the parapsychology researcher, public interest is not apt to wane as long as questions are unanswered. Additionally, people are discovering that despite the tremendous advances in science, technology and the comforts of living, man's problems are more numerous, not less. Consequently there is wider searching, and when man searches he's likely to turn toward a more inward or spiritual plane, even though ESP may in essence by physical.

Healthier still, in my opinion, is the vast interest of young people. Seeking to get away from the crushing technological plane, the outward indifference of much of society, many are deeply interested, or even involved in at least one aspect of the field with open-minded, analytical approaches.

Touring the college circuits week after week, I've seen strong indications of realization that drugs are the one foolproof way to destroy society, that the young people can seek inward awareness through meditation and introspection, using the mental approach without Dr. Leary's killing chemical approach. That aspect alone justifies public support.

The study of ESP has gone through two stages: the collection of data on spontaneous phenomena, such as the Shindo case, gathered from every source, and the experimental laboratory. Without design and intent, certainly, the latter stage has tended to stifle advancement of research, the exact opposite of its goal. The precise requirements of pure science—proof along each step of the ladder, and the traditional rigidity of the lab—work against chances of success.

In this field especially, science must not stay within four walls with a litter of mechanical devices, because the emotional factor, a key ingredient, is often left at the door. Emotions are suppressed and some of the significant data, such as deathlike images and accidental situations, involve emotional ties. Additionally, ESP responses, from my own experience, are easier to come by in a freewheeling atmosphere. Box the mind and it tends to stay boxed.

Of necessity, Dr. Rhine's early experiments were in the lab. His ESP cards were hardly complex. Only the data were complex and rocked the academic world, not unexpectedly. The former botanist was attacked shrilly by some, with hard calculation by others. His tests eventually withstood both philosophical and analytical barrages. ESP was coming of age and was awarded a degree of respectability.

The twenty-five cards displayed one of five symbols—a cross, a circle, a star, a square or two small parallel wavy lines. I first tried them in my early teens and if I was at all uncertain about the existence of psychic phenomena, Dr. Rhine's cards stilled any doubts.

The idea was, and still is, for one person to identify, by thought perception, the symbol of a card picked up, and concentrated on, by another person. There is visual separation, so facial expressions cannot be read. Mathematics, or even gambler's odds, rule that five hits could be discounted as roulette-wheel probables. Over that percentage is the claimed area of extrasensory perception. In Rhine's published research of tests with two assistants, separated by buildings, 558 hits were recorded out of a possibility of 1,850 chances. Mathematics challenged the findings but could not conclusively defeat them.

Later sophistication of tests with the ESP cards led Rhine to believe that some individuals had the capability of perceiving the order of the stacked cards without seeing them, even predicting their sequence following a shuffle. I have tried the latter test a number of times but have not been successful at it. However, I don't doubt that it is possible, and Rhine's statistics indicate the possibility beyond the mathematical probable.

From his entire battery of tests, Rhine concluded that there was a possibility of clairvoyance and precognition, as well as the high probability of thought perception.

A beginner's version of the Rhine tests to measure ESP sensitivity, primarily telepathy sensitivity, can be accomplished with an ordinary deck of playing cards. The tester removes one red card and one black card to even the number to fifty, then the cards are shuffled. A large book is opened and placed on the table as a screen between the tester and the subject, who has been provided with a sheet of paper, numbered to fifty.

On a signal of "ready" the tester concentrates about ten seconds on the color of the card he is holding up, blocked from the subject's view by the book. The subject then writes "red" or "black," depending on the signal he receives from the tester. Each new card is preceded by the "ready" signal. After the fifty cards have been run out, each placed face down in order of appearance, score can be counted by corresponding the deck with the subject's numbered sheet. Any score of thirty-five hits or higher indicates that more than pure chance was involved. It is not an exacting test but may provide ESP-sensitivity information if several runs of the cards indicate consistent scores of thirty-five or over.

Acceptance by science, in general, and the general public, could come about when parapsychologists are able to gather enough data in each area to conclusively prove that *psi,* that tangible intangible key to ESP, does indeed exist. The burden of this is seeking out not only those people thought to have ESP capabilities beyond the average, but correlating a wide range of experiences. With *psi* as reliable as a thistle, with a lunatic fringe involved in the field, and quackery rampant, it's a formidable but not hopeless task.

Most known "psychics" have been tested in various labs by experts or by the Society for Psychical Research in London, or its cousin in New York, the American Society for Psychical Research, and varied results were obtained. Summary of all the testing seems to be a hardly startling affirmation: yes, they are psychic. Bedeviling the experts is always the "why" and "how."

On two occasions I submitted to lab tests. Each time, within minutes, I felt a sharp decrease in whatever ESP capability I have. I believe it is a personal flaw, stemming from the non-lab nature of my work. Perhaps I should have been professional enough to overcome the mechanics or the lack of spontaneity, but I found it impossible. I struggled through the tests, knowing that I had a partial block. However, I will always gladly submit to testing on my home ground of the stage, doing what I normally do. In that role, within a few minutes, I'm not aware I'm being tested; my responses are normal and natural.

Astronauts or cosmonauts would probably be ideal laboratory test subjects. They have been conditioned to accept lab procedures and function naturally and normally while undergoing the most complicated scientific probings known to man. Doctrine and mechanics might not affect their psychic responses.

To me, one of the most intriguing, perhaps the most exciting, area of psychic phenomena has to do with field forces that are said to exist around all of us, extending beyond our physical bodies but related to them. These same *psi* fields are believed to exist around any living tissue, and even around certain "dead" tissue, linking us by fields to animal, vegetable and mineral.

Aura, as applied to parapsychology, means an emanation from bodies, animate or inanimate, supposedly caused by mental or physical magnetic forces. Our awareness of *aura,* in certain cases, is termed "field consciousness." According to this theory, we are conscious of a field force of some type that appears to be paranormal. Current work by physicists, not psychologists, may someday explain what these forces are, and how they work. Meanwhile, it is difficult to discount their existence.

In support of these theories, most people have encountered a field force at one time or another, in one way or another, attributing it to a "strange feeling." The force could have been purely psychic or physical and magnetic. The range of these forces and their categories remain practically unknown.

A think-tank in California was recently awarded a fifty-thousand-dollar federal grant for research into the field of consciousness of the philodendron, apparently a very sensitive plant. On the face of it, this would seem to be a senseless piece of research, but the ultimate goal is to decide whether or not the beautiful green-leafed *Araceae* can be of help in detecting aerial hijackers.

That some plants may have a "thought capacity" has been projected by polygraph expert Cleve Backster. Some years ago he attached two galvanic skin-response electrodes to the leaves of a philodendron in his office with the idea of burning a leaf for possible reaction on the lie detector. The plant reacted *before* he could strike the match. It *perceived his thought* and understood what might be a hostile gesture. Incredibly, the polygraph needle jumped.

Later tests included two philodendrons witnessing the "stomping death" of a third. Subsequently, when the "murderer" entered the room, the two surviving plants registered frantically on the polygraph.

To those who shake their heads at Backster's scientific findings, the question of the "green thumb" has to be posed. Why does one gardener have lush plants and foliage, while his neighbor next door, with the same earth, same light exposure, same fertilizer, grows a garden of weeds? Technique enters, but there are gardeners who "talk to their plants." Who is to say that there is not a sensitive response?

In storm prediction, the sensitivity of certain wildlife is found to be the equal of or better than the U.S. Weather Bureau. And how does a dog sense the demise of his master in a hospital five miles away, beginning to wail at almost the instant of death?

Research in ESP and *psi* will likely go far beyond the human mind. The theory that we are all part of our environment, daily carrying on an undiscovered relationship with it, is not so far-fetched. Neither is the theory that psychic phenomena are simply a part of the total nature of man.

PART II
THE POWER
OF SUGGESTION

[1]

Suggestion, for my specific purposes of entertainment, is the presentation of an idea to an individual, or group of individuals. It may or may not have a rationality to it. If it is accepted, it is accepted uncritically. If the person or persons do not respond to it, it is rationally dissolved. I say to a subject, "You're getting cold." Reason would tell him that there is absolutely no rational or physical cause for feeling chill. Yet, because of conditioning and uncritical response, he reacts. As my conviction grows, his chill grows.

If an individual sits with his eyes closed and is convincingly told that a heated half dollar is being placed on his forehead, sensors will show that his temperature rises slightly. Yet he knows that no one is sticking a red-hot coin between the eyes. It is but another example of our complete vulnerability to suggestion.

95

These, however, are natural responses. If you become engrossed in a book about the Arctic, if the descriptions of a howling wind and of vast fields of ice and snow are exceptional, you may well react. You may also find that your body temperature has been slightly lowered. By the same token, if someone enters a room saying, "My, it's hot in here," you suddenly become aware of heat that hadn't bothered you a moment before. Suggestion at work!

A timeless elementary psychology test is to select one hapless student prior to the next class, and have a few selected students tell him he doesn't look too well. Or ask him worriedly, "How do you feel, Jack?" Periodic reminders of his state of health, which happens to be superb, brings doubts. Soon he thinks he doesn't feel well.

Chain response can be triggered without any verbal prompting. During the two world wars, Army and Navy processing centers daily reported incidents of fainting on the inoculation lines. Two or three at a time, strapping men would flop over *before* the needle was inserted, responding to the suggestive sight of the syringe up the line.

Most humans are defenseless against suggestion in varying degrees. "Looks like you're putting on a little weight" can send people dashing to the scales even though they haven't gained a pound in a year. "Is your hair getting thin?" prompts a trip to the mirror. At dinner, one person can ruin an otherwise perfectly good meal by suggesting, "This soup tastes a little bitter, doesn't it? I hope the can was okay." The can was fine, but good-bye soup.

It is simple but baffling suggestion at work.

Through autosuggestion, with calm, tranquil imagery, I can lower my pulse rate to fifteen or eighteen beats a minute against the normal seventy-two. By holding that imagery, and for myself, by adding a total bluelike quality in a setting of green trees, I can easily maintain this languid metabolic rate. I don't say to myself, "My pulse is going down. I'm relaxing. I feel drowsy." That's the worn patter of impotent "self-hypnosis," as meaningless as reading tea leaves. Should anyone desire that input, it should be recognized as a crutch. It's worth no more than that.

If I change the imagery to red and bring running horses in, my pulse beat will rise rapidly. That is autosuggestion in its purest form. For some time the Russians have been using a similar method to train soldiers to minimize pain. The pain becomes a sensation of pressure or is divided up over different parts of the body.

Autosuggestion, or self-suggestion, is exactly what it implies —an internal communication with and between the mind and any part of the body, or the body as a whole. It is believed that we speak to ourselves, as infants, long before we learn to speak to others. If we are not mentally ill, no day goes by when we don't talk to ourselves, either verbally or mentally. Autosuggestion, then, is a directed, channeled form of internal communication with the mind as central control. It is normal and not paranormal.

With what little we have learned of it, and are learning, autosuggestion is an old-fashioned term already, and oversimplified. But no one has been able to come up with a better definition. Perhaps we should stay with it lest we be stuck with one of those staggering lab concoctions. But as a mind source power, it is almost totally unexplored and untapped, capable of masking or alleviating pain, reducing tensions without use of drugs, and possibly achieving potentials beyond our present comprehension. The manifestations are not "hypnotic." They are completely normal and natural.

Conviction is the key.

Suggestion has of course always been the keystone of "hypnosis." But beyond this manufactured sleep state, it is the natural daily persuasion used in every human contact. At home, in the office, at school; at play and work, at love-making, it is as much a part of our lives as "yes" and "no" responses.

In his book *Our Magic*, published in 1911, effects creator Nevil Maskelyne wrote: "Having induced a marked condition of mental receptivity, we cannot expect our subjects to conceive ideas other than those we create, either directly or by suggestion." Neither a "hypnotist" nor a clinical psychologist, Maskelyne was accurately analyzing techniques of mystifying audiences. At the same time, in a few simple words, he described the foundation for suggestibility.

The power of suggestion, or as the Russians now term it, the *science of suggestology*, has every indication that it can become a completely normal communication of the future, even though, in its ESP form, it will be nonverbal and telepathic.

Moving beyond the word "suggestion," the science of suggestology or suggestibility, in highest refinement, is based on the human ability to accept an idea and respond to it almost automatically, whether it is verbal or nonverbal. It is a normal response in most humans, often those who are highly individual, creative and often artistic. On responding, they will be totally awake—laughing, talking, normal in every sense.

Most people respond easily to suggestion. As a simple "homemade" experiment, tell a friend, very casually, "There's a red spot on your arm. Does it itch?"

First he'll look for the spot. Then he'll likely answer defensively, "You're crazy. There's no spot on my arm."

Keep looking down at his arm. "Oh?"

Your friend is now apt to be staring at the imaginary spot. He may begin to doubt his own eyes, even though he'll protest you're insane. If you glance away he may furtively scratch it. If you persist, reminding him of the external surface of his body, of which he is seldom conscious, he might begin to itch all over.

A more subtle experiment is to catch someone who is

whistling while engrossed in work. Do not attract his attention, but begin whistling another tune very softly. After a moment, increase the volume. Usually, he will shift to your tune without being aware he's done so. Later he'll probably declare, as part of an unconscious defense mechanism, that your tune was what he was whistling in the first place. He is a victim of your suggestion.

In terms of autosuggestion, become aware of the skin for a few minutes. Think of the possibility that your own arm might itch, perhaps the underpart of the other arm, and the area behind your knee. If you work at it, you can be tingling from head to toe in a minute. You'll have to reprogram yourself by thinking about something else.

As another example of suggestion, certain TV or radio commercials are mildly irritating. By calculation on Madison Avenue, they narrow your attention. You may try to ignore them. Can you?

Try not to think of the word "moonbeam" every time you see the word NIGHT pop up in the next paragraph.

Every time you see NIGHT *you will find yourself thinking of the word* "MOONBEAM."

So you can attempt to ignore the commercial but then the words simply impress themselves on an unconscious level. NIGHT. Or you can consciously react to the annoyance by making up your mind that you don't like the commercial and won't purchase the product. Ironically, the advertiser may be satisfied with your response. NIGHT. They have made some impression on you. Most likely, you'll forget the specific incident on a conscious level. Yet a few days later when you are shopping, you find yourself confronted with myriad brands of the product you'd like to purchase. NIGHT. You think to yourself, "They're probably all equally good, so I'll grab this one." Chances are extremely high that the brand you pick unthinkingly is the one that antagonized you a week earlier. NIGHT. You would have been better off remembering the earlier stimuli. But it hits you in a busy moment and life is too full of everyday happenings to bother with small things. NIGHT.

If you found yourself thinking "moonbeam" on reading NIGHT, the power of suggestion worked. Even if you fought against it, sternly rejecting the idea that some silly words on paper would force you to respond, it still worked. *To reject it, you had to think of it.* Additionally, the unconscious accepted it whether you liked it or not.

For me, professionally, suggestion functions with one person, ten or two hundred, and there isn't a "hypnotic" trance nor a candle flicker of mysticism in the whole house. Using only suggestion, tapping nothing but waiting imagination, I've had subjects seeing flying saucers or shivering in polar cold within two minutes, and audiences of six hundred dancing Irish jigs. I doubt that the few who saw the spinning saucers, got goosebumps or did the Donegal stomp were abnormal, although some might have been supersensitive to suggestion, as pliable as child's clay. They can be lumped with those very fortunate people (if there are any) who have seen the Hindu rope trick.

In this, the most splendid form of imagery, the fakir supposedly throws a rope into the air and his assistant climbs to the top and disappears. The fakir, knife in teeth, climbs up after him and vanishes. It becomes a "full setting," in the beautiful parlance of a Houdini or Great Thurston. Suddenly parts of the assistant's body begin to fall from the air—a head, a leg, an arm. The fakir climbs back down to pick up pieces of the body, tossing them into a trunk. He finally closes it, utters some mumbo-jumbo, and then opens it. Out hops the smiling assistant. Blackstone did it on the stage in a modified form, and Thurston had his version of it.

Suggestibility has long been a theory in the case of the fakir's spell, and enchanting craftsmanship did it for Messrs. Blackstone and Thurston. Magic audiences enter with a dare in their eyes but quickly succumb to the childlike need within us all.

When a lady is sawed in half, bits of cloth flying through the air, the sound of the blade whirring through meat and bone, the elements are overwhelmingly suggestive. And the audience has already been conditioned, unconsciously, by simply relating to the word *magic*. Although the majority of the adults know for a fact that no lady is being sliced, they will still wince; many will close their eyes. Their imagination, so powerful that it cannot be thwarted, has been triggered. They can almost feel that shining blade as it grinds through bone.

The late Charles Carter, investigating secrets of Oriental sorcery in the early thirties, wrote: "Certain it is that in the hills of Simla, the atmosphere is extremely rarefied; deep inhalations of pure oxygen affect the brain and so produce hallucinations easily influenced by adroit operators." Certain, also, is that hallucination itself is real magic and mystery beyond the wildest dreams of a Great Carter or Thurston.

It has been claimed that a photographer once snapped the rope trick, positive that he had at last caught the astounding and legendary feat. However, when the picture was developed, the fakir and his assistant were still standing on earth, and the rope was curled around the fakir's arm. Nobody was climbing; nothing had happened. It was all in the photographer's imagination. The topper to this story is that no one, to my knowledge, has ever seen that particular photograph nor identified the photographer by name. More than that, the probability of an entire mass of people repeatedly hallucinating, day to day, week to week, must be questioned. The rope trick remains a fairy tale, a "Jack and the Beanstalk," at least to me, until proven otherwise.

However, imagery born of suggestibility is momentarily as powerful and true, in the mind, as hemp tied firmly in the air. It isn't even necessary to take a trip to Simla or draughts of rarefied air. *Harvey*, a play about a huge imaginary rabbit, was a Broadway hit for years. The rabbit never appeared on stage, but the leading character, first played by Frank Fay, talked with him as if he existed. Some people in the audience became so involved that they forgot they weren't supposed to see Harvey. Their imagination did the rest. Fay reported that he was asked, quite seriously, "Wherever did you get a rabbit that big?"

[2]

With imagination as the key, with the power of suggestion as the tool, I stage and guide charades, intensifying them to the point where the subject discards his everyday role. The drifting daydream is put on like a cloak. It all becomes real. The mind, being very capable of a daydream, is also capable of "going to the moon." It does not require someone with psychic powers to come up on the wavelengths.

Not long ago, in a night-club setting, I suggested the role of "moon people" to a pair of college students. I did not "hypnotize" them. I simply got their attention and after a moment of conditioning, manipulated their imaginations. In a few minutes, they were talking animatedly. I guided them to discuss how they lived out there, or up there.

In situations like this, what comes out in the cross talk between two "moon people" is of course gibberish to everyone else, a fascinating phenomenon in itself. One, though, acts as interpreter and explains what goes on aboard that poetic satellite. That person *imagines* that he or she can interpret the gibberish. Sometimes it seems earnest enough to be real. It is pure invention. In other shows I often ask the interpreter to inquire of the "moon man" how many sexes exist on that cheery ball. Invariably, and unexplainably, the answer will be four. I haven't the faintest idea why, or what triggers that precise number.

Suddenly, in this particular show, I saw the "moon person" turn to the interpreter and ask a question in gibberish. The other people on the stage began laughing, then the audience burst into laughter. Because I had been more interested in audience reaction than what was occurring on stage at this point, the crowd was ahead of me.

Puzzled, I looked at them and in turning back to the subjects, saw the interpreter pointing toward a stairway which was off to the side of the club. He answered in gibberish, dropping his role of interpreter and becoming a concerned friend. The moon inhabitant then left his chair and began to walk toward the stairway.

It dawned on me that he'd asked directions to the men's room.

The audience quieted down as they saw the subject leave the stage and head for the steps. They looked back at me. I was dumbstruck. It had never happened before. So far as I knew, there was no way to communicate something of this sort in *bleee-be-da-ba-g aga-boob.* Yet it had been done.

It also occurred to me that in going downstairs the subject might well meet someone who would speak to him in a friendly tone. His possible reply in "moon" gibberish, *booo-agggga-goo,* could bring about gent's-room bewilderment, even a hard punch in the nose.

I ran after him, caught him and reprogrammed him, letting him proceed to his urgent mission as other than a "moon man."

The fact that nature sent him toward the W.C. is entirely explainable because he wasn't in any sleeping "trance" nor in a special physical or mental condition. But his ability to communicate his need in "satellite" language is beyond my knowledge to this date. Undoubtedly, given the right circumstances, it will happen again.

This type of phenomenon, I believe, evolves straight from psychodrama. If a group of closely knit people play charades for about an hour, suggestibility usually increases to the point that when a scene or idea is projected by the person doing the pantomime, he or she will function automatically, submerging into the role and expanding it without great thought.

I have observed charades that have been close to telepathy,

although the players were completely unaware of having crossed over into another form of communication.

[3]

One of the masters of suggestibility is Arthur Godfrey. Though his audiences on radio and TV have been in the millions, Godfrey often sounds as if he were talking to a single person. Some of his commercials have been classics. No other entertainer has been as skilled in the use of audio communication. His tapes are an education in salesmanship alone and I owe much to his techniques and to his personal encouragement.

For different goals, though involving salesmanship, too, evangelist Billy Graham is a master at "holding" an audience. There is a cadence in his voice, a build toward dramatic peaks, and his appearance is compelling. Had he decided to enter politics instead of evangelism, the possibility of Washington residence would not be remote. I once claimed, on the air, that Graham was a "master hypnotist," using the term in reference to his abilities to verbally "hold" a crowd. A ruffled member of Graham's staff called me to complain. However, Graham himself had, years before, admitted his knowledge of audience control on Art Linkletter's CBS *House Party*.

Another widely known and skilled practitioner is Bishop Fulton J. Sheen. It is evident that he has a thorough understanding of the suggestibility phenomenon. His eyes, the structure of his face, the firm yet soothing quality of his voice, and his expert timing combine to produce a "holding" effect on audiences, whether live or TV. In the case of both Billy Graham and Bishop Sheen, their abilities are used for the betterment of mankind.

My own techniques are somewhat different, tailored for amusement, and directed toward immediate "hold" on an audience to afford participation. I'm hardly a compelling figure and, unfortunately, lack Bishop Sheen's hypnotic eyes. I've been told that I look something like Mr. Spock, from the planet Vulcan, of the TV series *Star Trek*. I find that flattering. Vulcan sounds as if it might be an interesting place to live on, and such a background would undoubtedly add to mentalizing, but I have to do it the hard verbal or telepathic way.

At one point in my concerts I discuss my beliefs that there is no special state of "hypnosis," no need for fabricating a sleeplike trance. I confess that I once not only practiced what I believed to be so-called "hypnosis," but ardently fostered the trance concept. I tell the audience that my references to "hypnosis," both historically and as I practiced it, are in the framework of the past. This is also why I use quotation marks when dealing with the subject.

I then attempt to explain what is known of suggestibility, in which no trance is involved, and how we are all extremely prone to it. In this sense, we are imaginatively carried away with the actors and story of a good film, involving ourselves in it, losing the fact that it is fabricated on a chemical strip. We grip the seat and feel a surge of adrenaline during the chase in *The French Connection*. We are lost in it, responding to it, and we're far from "hypnotized." In somewhat the same way, I cause individuals to respond to suggestion without the induction of a trance.

At that point I invite volunteers from the audience for demonstrations of suggestibility. While most "hypnotists" will invite a dozen or so, hoping to find one or two who will be extra responsive, I've discovered the opposite is warranted. It isn't unusual for me to have ninety people onstage when I only ask for twenty-five or thirty chairs to be filled. The conditioning has already taken place. In fact, I think that by asking for a large number I fulfill the apparent encouragement factor of "safety in numbers." Filling the thirty chairs, I request that the others remain standing rather than send them back to their seats. Contrary to a long-held "hypnosis" belief, subjects do not have to feel relaxed to respond to suggestion.

It doesn't seem readily possible that in a matter of fleeting seconds a person onstage can cause strangers to forget their names, verbally lock their hands or clamp their eyelids shut.

I'll ask a man to step forward. "Are you wide awake?"

"Yes," he'll answer.

"Are you in a trance?"

"No."

Then I pause and change tone to subtly emphasize something I want to plant. I say, "You know, we can forget things in everyday life quite easily." I pass my hand across the front of his face.

He knows there is some significance to what I said, something unusual about the hand gesture, but he doesn't know what it is. The "plant" succeeds.

"Do you go to school?"

"No."

"Work?"

"Yes."

"Where do you live?"

"Peoria Heights."

I pause again, for perhaps three or four seconds, and then ask, in a meaningful way, spacing the words, "By the way, what is your name?"

He cannot remember it. He is keying back to the significant plant; he has been waiting for the question and has obeyed the suggestion. He is not "asleep-awake." He is wide awake.

In a theater in Pittsburgh, I worked this particular demonstration with an audience volunteer. He stood frowning, perplexed. I turned my back and the audience saw him reach into his coat pocket for his wallet, hoping to read his name off credit cards. I turned again quickly. "Your hand is locked in that pocket. You can't remove it." The hand was, for a moment, paralyzed by the motor responses. But this gentleman was not in a trance. Yet he was responding uncritically to an irrational suggestion.

As far as it is possible, I induce the responsive condition by natural references. Prior to setting up the "polar" atmosphere, I may say, "Wow, it's chilly in here." I fake a shiver. "I'm almost freezing. We've got a problem with the air conditioning tonight. But bear with us. We've called for a technician."

A few minutes later, having planted the "cold" idea, I'll proceed to attack the waiting response of the subjects with the hard suggestion that it is indeed freezing. Often, one or two will go to the curtains and gather folds about them.

Exactly what prompts response to an obviously irrational suggestion is not known. My own theory, admittedly a guess, is that the response is simply a normal extension of the everyday examples coupled with the sudden harnessing of imagination. *The response stops instantly unless the imagination is geared.* Once stimulated, it knows few boundaries. Expertly guided, suggestion-imagination is a miraculous mental vehicle.

Imagination, triggered by suggestion, is quite capable of controlling physical direction. The simplest test is to have a subject stand in front of me. I tell him to close his eyes and imagine that he is standing at the edge of a high building; street and traffic are twenty floors below. After a moment he'll begin to sway normally and naturally. I can then suggest that he fall backwards to me to safety. Invariably, if he is responding imaginatively to the idea that he is inches from the ledge, a sickening plunge beneath him, the suggestion will tilt him back into my arms. Every adult and most children have, at one time or another, looked down from a great height. It takes very little to freshen that vivid memory if the eyes are closed. This was one of the early Vasiliev suggestibility experiments.

However, environmental hazards easily trigger imagination. If a board five feet long and two feet wide is placed on the floor, a subject will usually walk it without concern, moving confidently, keeping his balance. Place the same board between two buildings and the subject may refuse to walk it. If he does agree, there is a possibility that he'll fall. Yet the physical characteristics of the board have not changed. There has been a change in attitude prompted by an imaginative stimulation.

While it is not an absolute rule, it appears that when imagination and the will are in conflict, as demonstrated by the board test, imagination will usually win.

I've taken this type of test to a more sophisticated degree on several occasions. On a Johnny Carson show I marked a card within a deck of cards and then handed the pack to another guest, asking TV personality Virginia Graham to please stand and close her eyes. A staff member stood behind her. I proceeded to call off the cards and when the marked card was reached, Miss Graham toppled on mental order. She was not aware, at the moment, why she'd fallen backwards. *Suggestion had been mentally implanted.* The demonstration is on NBC tape for those who are skeptical. Dr. Vasiliev conducted similar experiments.

I once walked up to a standing subject and requested that he stiffen his leg. Moving away, I told him that he could not bend it. He lumbered and limped all over the stage. I released him, and he immediately said, "Now I can bend it."

I nodded. "That's very true, but the condition has been transferred to your left leg." He took a step forward and found that one rigid.

Playing a date on the Italian cruise ship *Victoria*, on a voyage to the Caribbean, I made one subject take off her shoes and then replace them on the opposite feet. I requested her to stand up and walk.

"Are you certain you have your shoes on the right way?"

"Yes, I'm certain."

"Do they feel all right?"

"They feel fine."

All the while, she was practically falling down.

Suggestibility rips through inhibitions and occasionally makes me wonder if all of us do not have "parrotlike" abilities that we suppress—photographic and audio impressions that are stored in our memory banks, never brought to life until the charade is stimulated. One night at the Embers I questioned a subject about his TV-watching habits. He said that he always watched *Gunsmoke.* I replied, "In a few minutes you'll be Chester." Soon he was walking through the audience calling for "Mr. Dillon" in the distinctive accent of Dennis Weaver. He even walked like Weaver. He apparently was enjoying the brief period as Matt Dillon's deputy because he stopped at several tables to sign autographs. I examined them later. They were signed "Chester."

The ability to not only take on characterization but create it constantly surfaces. In at least one phase of all my concerts I attempt to bring out creativity. At Kutztown State Teachers College in Pennsylvania, last fall, I told a subject that within a few minutes he would rise from his chair and request my microphone because a very important cause was on his mind: he wanted to raise funds to feed the "starving bloodhounds of Upper Srednikan in the White Hills of Russia." He listened intently while I explained that they lived on a diet of Limburger cheese and Chanel No. 5. I impressed upon him that it was a terribly serious mission.

The audience awaited his readiness to make the speech while I went on with another routine. About four minutes later he arose and took my mike. No one laughed. I think the audience wondered if a person could seriously sustain what was a ludicrous subject and carry it off without self-consciousness. A seasoned performer, a comedian, could do it. This subject was a student. But very often, inhibitions and self-consciousness are lost in the group setting. The student had been a part of the large group onstage, identifying with them, and fortifying from them. Knowing what the auditorium reaction would eventually be, I had instructed him to stamp his foot if the audience did annoy him. He began to make the speech, his face deadly serious, his voice carrying earnest conviction. It was utterly ridiculous as well as hilarious. The audience began to laugh. He stamped his foot and they roared.

In the spring I'd done the same routine while entertaining a dentists' convention. My subject, a young man, pleaded emotionally for the dogs, exposing what might have been a personal issue—that dentists were making huge sums of money nowadays and could well afford to share some with the dogs of Upper Srednikan. He borrowed a hat and began going through the audience, which was now in stitches.

Deep conviction at work, sprung by suggestibility, is rather awesome to witness, sometimes provoking disturbing reflections. At St. Lawrence University in Canton, New York, I told a group of about eight football players that the dean of students, a man named Kirkpatrick, would enter the auditorium and come up onstage, but that this "Kirkpatrick" was really an imposter and should not be allowed to remain inside. About five minutes later the real Dean Kirkpatrick came down the aisle, and although they knew him well, they forcibly removed him. It was well below zero outside and he entered a second time. The subjects headed for him again. I ended it.

Visual response is but another phase of the suggestibility phenomenon. On occasion I'll carry what looks like a dozen pairs of eyeglasses onstage, and in setting up the demonstration, point out that these particular "glasses" will cause great distortion, so that the subjects will see one another as though looking into "fun-house" mirrors at carnivals. After I place the "glasses" on their foreheads, asking them please not to touch them, the subjects look at one another and begin to break up. It is interesting to observe how they handle this suggestion. Some claim the others have the heads of giraffes, eyes like headlights or noses like bananas. They are remembering what they have seen in similar true distortions. On completing the test, I stick a finger through the frames, showing both the subjects and the audience that there are no lenses.

Another version of sight response is to hand two subjects, seated closely, a single magazine, usually an issue of the pictorial type. I tell one subject that the pictures on the left-hand page are sad or poignant; and that the ones on the right-hand page are very funny. The other subject is given opposite instructions. The contrast, as each studies the same page, is startling. At Lycoming College in Williamsport, Pennsylvania, this test ended in an argument between the two readers, the more aggressive one ripping a page out.

Sound response to suggestibility is equally interesting. If a piano happens to be onstage, I often tell the subjects that I will play something by Chopin, perhaps the Étude, Opus 10, No. 3, the theme song from the film *The Magnificent Obsession* which I happen to like, but that as they hear it they will react with disgust. The rendition will be off key, full of discords. However, if I play "Chopsticks" it will sound classic, rendered beautifully.

I begin to play. Chopin causes some subjects to place their hands over their ears, others to groan. One girl, probably a classics lover, actually lowered the piano lid on my fingers. When I segue into "Chopsticks" the subjects sit back, enthralled.

Of all the senses, taste and smell are the easiest to distort. I don't do it often, for obvious reasons, but have handed an onion to a subject with his eyes closed, telling him that it is an apple.

"Good apple, huh?"

"Great."

The discovery is not so great. This test, however, will not work, or has not worked for me, if the subject has visual register coupled with a violent dislike of raw onions. Response cannot be forced against the knowing will.

Sometimes I end the suggestibility portion of the concert by telling the group onstage that one particular chair will burst into flames on signal. At a Knights of Columbus benefit in Union, New Jersey, a man dashed backstage for a fire extinguisher. At another concert a lady grabbed a pitcher of water off a table and tossed it, splashing the front row and dousing some expensive furs. I safeguard it now by ending the phase in another manner if water is available onstage.

[4]

On a summer's night long ago, at the Brant's Beach Yacht Club in New Jersey, I told the subjects onstage that they would see flying saucers. A portion of the sky was visible. I was performing on the screened-in yacht-club porch. Soon a number of the subjects saw unidentified flying objects skirting the heavens. Several ran to phones and were convincing enough to call out both the police and fire departments. The aftermath was rather embarrassing. Explanations of this sort of thing to police tend to bè awkward.

At any rate, much later I could truthfully answer Dr. Jay Allan Hynek, professor of astronomy at Northwestern University, when he contacted me about this area of the suggestibility phenomenon. He was scheduled to speak on UFO's before a science convention and had certain questions about the possibility of suggestion weighing heavily in some flying-saucer sightings. Highly regarded in his field, Dr. Hynek was involved in tracking Sputnik, the first Soviet space satellite, for the United States government, and has since devoted much time to UFO research.

The astronomer has a theory that if UFO's have approached this planet they might possibly be coming through from another galaxy, not within our universe, and that these intelligences are "passing through," perhaps accidentally, perhaps exploring. His theory was previously advanced by the National Investigations Committee on Aerial Phenomena, a large private group of prominent aviation figures. The committee includes aircraft pilots as well as space scientists.

Accepting the fact that a certain percentage of sightings by reputable people of sound mind, mostly experienced pilots, cannot be explained, Dr. Hynek believes that the large majority of sightings are completely false and doubts that any UFO has ever landed on the "earth planet." In this, he agrees with the *Scientific Study of Unidentified Flying Objects*, the report of an Air Force–sponsored commission headed by Dr. Edward U. Condon, professor of physics at the University of Colorado.

Findings of the careful Condon commission indicated that the overwhelming majority of reported sightings could be explained by visual distortions of completely normal aerial activity—aircraft and weather balloons to test atmospheric conditions. Illusion was given its due; fantasy and pure invention figured into the tens of thousands of flying-saucer incidents. Predictably, the Condon report was ignored by a host of UFO buffs and the "nut" fringe of the occult. Nothing could be more tailor-made for the occultists than Martians in silver suits scooting about in saucers and port-holed shining metallic sausages from Saturn.

Hynek was interested in the contagion of sightings, possibly prompted by self-suggestion or guided suggestibility, as occurred in the famous Orson Welles radio program of the 1930's. He was also interested in the interaction of groups under such conditions.

I agreed that a small percentage of the sightings might possibly be explained, or could be identified, in psychological terms, and offered to "stage" a sighting for his observation. He came up to TV station CJOH in Ottawa, where I tape my syndicated show, on a selected night.

Conditioning fourteen subjects, I told them that when we went to "black" for the commercial, they would return to the audience, dress warmly and then proceed outside the studio. Cameras had been set up outdoors, one of which would monitor the demonstration for the studio audience. I assured the subjects that when I came out and dropped a handkerchief, they would see three flying objects. Assisting in the test was news director Max Keeping from CJOH. His job was to interview the subjects, on camera, before and during the "sighting."

Along with Hynek and the studio audience, I watched the

subjects as we went to black for the commercial break. They dutifully returned to their seats, collected coats and gloves and then filed out into the night where Keeping was waiting. He began to question them about UFO's, and most expressed great skepticism.

I watched for a moment and then went outdoors to join them, Dr. Hynek following. The night was clear, icy cold. Stars were out. Mingling with them near the reporter, I pulled out the handkerchief, wiped my forehead with it and then dropped it. In a few seconds the fourteen subjects were sighting three flying saucers, pointing up and discussing them with Keeping. Skepticism had vanished.

One man rushed back into the studio, asking permission to use the phone to report UFO's. Studio personnel, briefed on what was occurring, refused his request. He returned outside, bitterly denouncing the studio employees for their apathy.

I then said, in a loud voice, that it appeared to me that one of the saucers was descending and that it would probably hover over the station within a few minutes. Two of the subjects began running across the snowy field toward the highway. I yelled, "Release," and they turned back; the other twelve subjects responded to the same signal.

Keeping began asking them about the saucers. Uniformly, the subjects either laughed at him or questioned his sanity. No one had seen "flying saucers."

Dr. Hynek was very interested to know exactly what they had seen. We all returned inside, out of subfreezing weather, and I suggested that the fourteen subjects back into their imaginative mental discovery. They responded in considerable detail including descriptions of shapes and designs of the UFO's. The colors varied; some saw yellow saucers and some saw green. Notably, no subject saw more than three saucers, the exact number I had suggested.

Later that night the astronomer concluded that suggestibility had played a much larger role in UFO sightings, where more than one person was involved, than previously thought. People had hallucinated saucers or huge metal cigars. It was not a distortion of reality but a sighting of "nothing." What triggered the hallucination? The answer to that would be as complex as any Martian visitor.

In the case of the fourteen subjects in Ottawa, they responded in the heat of the experiment and afterward, but in a comparatively short time they would have realized what had happened, as with all cases of suggestibility. The psychodrama keyed by suggestion is never permanent.

Individuals who continue to report "private" incidents with UFO's, as though selected by that other intelligence as contact person for the "earth planet," have to be suspect. There is no physical evidence to back up their sightings. The attention given to them or the commitment made to themselves on the initial sighting probably forces them on. Nonetheless, they are quite capable of contagion within a group, as is the person who genuinely hallucinates and genuinely believes he has spotted a spaceship from another galaxy.

[5]

Other than Adolf Hitler's madness, one of the first and most dramatic examples of mass suggestibility in modern times is Orson Welles's Mercury Theater radio presentation "The War of the Worlds," first performed on October 30, 1938, over the CBS network. Only on radio could "The War of the Worlds" have created such mass hysteria; only the genius of a Welles, relating the fictional landing of a Martian spaceship in New Jersey, could have made it work. The realism of his script and presentation, combined with sound effects, played directly into ready and willing imaginations.

The people who actually began to believe that the United States had been invaded from another planet were not naïve or particularly gullible. Those who had no doubts at all, convinced that bulbous, sulfuric heads were among us, simply possessed a greater degree of imagination. They included college professors and newspapermen. Obviously, people who tuned in late were more receptive. Listening to the tapes, a few minutes into the show I got the feeling that it was a live news broadcast—which, for the sake of realism, was Welles's intent. The "you are there" technique is an image stimulant.

To reconstruct briefly Welles's control of human imagination that night—and I doubt he had any idea of the frontier he had crossed or the silent machinery of suggestibility that he activated—there was a readiness for acceptance. It had been a dull run of weeks and months, and historically, incidents of this sort usually take place in times of doldrums. Besides, a certain amount of unplanned conditioning had occurred. Imaginations and natural curiosity had been whetted over the years by articles in newspapers and such magazines as *Popular Mechanics* and *Popular Science*, by elaborate and imaginative drawings of spaceships and Martians, by "Buck Rogers" and pulp science fiction. The moon and other planets were visible, possibly inhabited by creatures. A key element by this time was that man was flying. He could even fly from continent to continent, witness Charles Lindbergh. Beyond that—who knew? Projection, then as now, was not difficult.

So when a fictitious reporter, mike in hand, approached the spaceship in New Jersey to give an on-the-spot description, broadcast remote from where it was all happening, the elements of suggestibility were lined up like psychic cars in a midnight train. Any gaps could be filled, even expanded, by average and normal imagination.

As the reporter got closer and closer, describing the intense heat, gasping and finally losing his voice, no wonder a portion of the audience swallowed Martians and swallowed hard.

Suddenly there was dead silence, and then Welles, at master control back at the station, said, "Come in, come in, where are you?"

That capped it.

One listener, later interviewed by the New York *Daily News*, had climbed to the roof of a low building and described events that were taking place across the river to an awed crowd gathered below. "I see the lights increasing and some more have landed."

He cannot be faulted. He was not an idiot, nor was he gullible. In his mind he "saw" those lights. He *saw* more spaceships landing. Without doubt, he was stimulated by the crowd below because he began to serve a role in the entire psychodrama. Suggestively speaking, his imagination was reinforced by the crowd and consequently he saw more of the events in New Jersey, from his Manhattan rooftop, as he went along.

That Welles did not really know the possible consequences of stepping across onto an unknown plain comparatively larger than earth itself was demonstrated both that evening and later. I remember awakening one early schoolday in the forties and listening to Prescott Robinson, on New York's WOR, announce that "The War of the Worlds" had been re-created the previous night in Venezuela. At broadcast's end the listeners were informed it was only fiction. Their fright and then rage ended with the burning of the station and the death of two announcers.

Another and different example of group suggestibility comes from my own home. I was a small child when I first heard my father's story of "the Headless Man," and since he has not changed a word of it, not even an inflection, in thirty years, I take it to be true. *The truth lies in what he thought he saw.*

With two teen-age friends, my father went to visit a relative in a nearby town in Pennsylvania. They walked the distance of about twelve miles, since they didn't have a car or horse. During the afternoon they were warned to leave well before dark, otherwise they might meet "the Headless Man" on the bridge en route home. This warning had been issued on other visits, but my father had never heeded it. Neither had he ever crossed the bridge at night.

The boys laughed it off and it was almost dark when they started for home. By the time they reached the bridge it was total night. Walking abreast, the two friends to my father's left, they were talking about other things, but it is obvious they were mindful, unconsciously, of what they might encounter.

My father then became aware of a sound or vibration to his right and looked. Keeping precise pace with them was a man dressed in black and seemingly devoid of a head. My father glanced to his left and saw that his friends were running across the bridge, having already spotted the night walker. My father ran too.

He maintains that he did *see* "the Headless Man," and his friends, one of them still living, firmly backs him up. I don't deny that they "saw" something, but the picture, in my opinion, was sent from the unconscious, similar to my own reception of an image over a darkened theater, or on the surface of a glass of water.

Unless a farmer was playing a prank, my father and his friends had suffered momentary group hallucination. It is a not uncommon, though sometimes frightening, phenomenon.

[6]

People are suggestible in different settings. A scientist may not be suggestible in an auditorium, but may be very receptive when he is alone, or in close rapport with a single person. An actress, on the other hand, capable of great flights of imagination, can be carried away in the midst of thousands.

Emotions, of course, play a part. They lend to suggestibility. The emotional "*Sieg heil*'s" at SS rallies in Germany were like waves mounting in a storm, pushed by the winds of suggestion, crashing higher and higher. The skilled controller can manipulate them as if they were musical instruments.

Exactly what part suggestibility played in unleashing Hitler's madness cannot be easily determined. However, the estimate is considerable. Beyond his ability as a spellbinding speaker, he apparently understood the power of suggestion and how to use it to sway millions, bringing them to the roaring "*Sieg heil*'s."

Too, he knew something of "hypnotic" techniques, having sat in on more than two hundred demonstrations. The average person, unless interested in the field or making a clinical study, would not attend more than a dozen sessions in a lifetime. Hitler's early tutor was a German expert named Eric Jan Hanussen, who was reportedly liquidated in 1934.

Hanussen was an intriguing man with a long criminal record. He was a noted entertainer, columnist, soothsayer, "clairvoyant," opera producer, song writer, and counselor to some of the Nazi social élite.

In the months before Hitler took power, Hanussen's astrology column repeatedly predicted "the Coming of the Messiah," though he didn't name the housepainter as Germany's new Saviour. Once Hitler emerged, Hanussen began to predict events of the Nazi party in various cities, days or even hours before they would occur. Those accurate prophecies are not too surprising, since he was privy to many secrets and his predictions appear to have followed a careful plan. Soon they proved fatal to the seer. Because of his knowledge, influence and prestige, Hanussen was a target on June 30, 1934, in a quiet country setting. Other executions of "dangerous people" were carried out that same night in Berlin and Bavaria. Hanussen had served his purpose.

Although I don't understand German, a certain "attention-holding" cadence can be established in listening to tapes of Hitler's voice. In films of his speeches, either by day or night, objects that reflect light can be seen behind him. I doubt that they were there by accident. As the speeches mount, lights catch them. They flash. Hitler was the central controller, using mass suggestibility that eventually made armies roll across Europe. It is tragic that many of the dynamic figures of history have been dictator types and that many have employed the techniques of mass suggestibility, coming by it naturally or guided by experts. A current model in world politics, almost paralleling Hitler in persuasion, is Cuba's Fidel Castro.

After a Manhattan concert, in which I described Castro's

techniques as "extremely suggestible," capable of holding people in a verbal palm, a *New York Times* reporter, a Cuban, came backstage to say, "I know exactly what you mean. I listened to him one day in the square in Havana and didn't realize until he had finished that I had been standing there almost five hours and was completely soaked from rain."

That night I'd had subjects onstage for an hour and ten minutes but they thought they'd only been up there for five minutes. They were not in a trance. They'd been awake, as the *Times* reporter was, as Hitler's audiences were, as Welles's radio listeners were. The time distortion, the acceptance of lies and Martians, was the result of being trapped in an imaginative response.

The response can easily be turned physical. During the period of the great religious revivals that began in the United States around 1804, many participants, particularly in Tennessee and Kentucky, fell to the ground, apparently senseless, while listening to the preacher. Another form of the epidemic hysteria was the "jerking exercise," which began with the arms and then extended to the neck and shoulders. A third variety that appeared at the revivals was a "whirling exercise" in which the carried-away sinners whirled like tops. It would begin with one or two participants and then spread throughout the open-air meetings. Response to suggestion is at the bottom of the religious manifestations of the Holy Rollers, the Shakers and the New Lights.

In 1922 a mass hysterical response occurred at a high school in North Carolina. Cadets were parading on a hot spring afternoon and four keeled over. Several girls then fainted in the grandstand. Before the suggested reaction ran its bizarre course, an estimated sixty people had toppled.

In the broad aspect, involving both mental and physical responses with all its potential for good, guided suggestibility or suggestology has the potential for incomparable, paralyzing evil when used to sway masses.

The Chicago riots at the 1968 Democratic convention did not *just happen*. Neither did the riots at Kent State University. They were guided by central control of agitators expertly using the power of suggestion. The crowds, after a point, were unknowingly responding in a hypersuggestible manner. They were wide awake, functioning normally in every sense except that of a rational mind.

Most of the high school and college students in both places will at first angrily deny any psychic influence, simply because they were not aware of the careful and gradual mind conditioning that had taken place prior to the riots. Nor were they particularly aware of the inciting key words being used by the roughly two dozen organizers or controllers, most of them men in their fifties.

During the four days of Chicago some rather old but still sophisticated conditioning techniques were employed, although they were outwardly the picture of innocence, youthful exuberance and pleasure. Mixed in with the rock music, dancing and some use of narcotic stimulants were key inflammatory phrases—*mind plants that would bloom at the proper moments.* Mass movement, heat, noise and racing pulses need little but the power of suggestion, in any setting, to produce mob reactions.

Dancing has long been used as a conditioner. The war dances of the American Indian were not intended to calm the braves. They were drummed out for the more efficient use of the tomahawk. African tribal dances are often purely "suggestive," in more than a sexual sense. Long ago they were used to "psyche up" the warriors prior to battle, to build morale and a single-minded purpose. Football pep rallies have much the same purpose.

Some of the marches in Chicago were subtle conditioners, notable for the chanting of key suggestive phrases such as, chiefly, "Get the pigs." Other marches, in contrast, were subdued and nonsuggestive, probably indicating that no ultramilitant controller was in the line.

Similar to dancing, marches provide a mass body, generating a unified instrument which can be, if purposely programmed, used for mind control. Introduction of a symbolic chant tends to bind the mass. The "Ho-Ho-Ho Chi Minh" of the Chicago streets, an import from German student demonstrations, was symbolic rather than suggestive.

As to phrasing, in any type of conquest, football or war or riots, there may not be enough time for critical thought, so numbers or symbolic words are substituted to ignite a "spontaneous" reaction. In the case of some disturbances, current and years back, reaction was not "spontaneous" at all as it affected the subjects, or properly, the victims. It was programmed.

Once the conditioning is accomplished and the mob ignited, the job of the professional controller is to sustain the riot action by continued use of the power of suggestion, moving in to toss more verbal napalm where the emotional fires are dying out. Central control is necessary. Without it, few riots will last longer than several hours. Like an explosion, they tend to splash to the outer part of the human circle, diminishing in intensity.

As part of a study of mass psychology, narrowing eventually to mob control, done as a personal interest, I interviewed numerous students who were involved at Kent State. I also talked to a number involved in Chicago. Roughly one half of my appearances each year are on college campuses and most times there's a lively give-and-take bull session after the concerts. But having this weekly, monthly contact with students, I could not clearly understand the sudden shift to violence in 1968 and 1969. I did make a guess that some of it had to be controlled.

The President's commission and other, independent reports affirm there had been tension in the Kent State community long before the actual outbreak. On occasion it had reached the point of terror. Sometimes baskets of broken glass were dumped on the heads of pedestrians, setting the stage for counterreaction.

Before it peaked, the conditioners again employed the dancing, rock music and key wordings of Chicago. The results, of course, were tragic. But in my findings they were predictable and inevitable as long as the conditioners, and controllers, were permitted to operate. To deny them that right is another matter, perhaps without solution. Yet as one who professionally practices "suggestibility" and knows its power, I tend to agree with Justice Oliver Wendell Holmes that no one has the right to yell "Fire!" in a crowded theater if there is none. The situations are parallel; civil liberties are involved in both.

After fomenting experimental riots on college stages, using only the power of suggestion to create the climate for violence, simply to prove a point, I've had students come backstage to say, "Now I know what you mean when you say 'suggestive' techniques were used in Chicago [or Kent State]. I was there and see the similarity in approach."

This does not mean that the students were not willing, even desirous of participation, of *gladly* joining in violence. It does mean that the emotions of the participants were calculatedly programmed and that many of their responses were totally uncritical. The students were, in brief, "used."

I'm fully aware of the peace-movement passions and issues involved, of the bitter disappointments, of the purpose and steadfast beliefs. I'm sympathetic to them. Yet, as a steady practitioner in the use of the power of suggestion, I also know that Chicago, Kent State, Berkeley, and other examples of student disruption that led to self-defeating violence could not have occurred without programmed incitement. The high school march on Mayor Lindsay's office in New York did not "just happen" on the spur of the moment. The late Senator Everett Dirksen was quoted, ". . . some of the men in that group were the same faces as in Chicago."

Following the August 1970 meeting of state university executives in Chicago, a meeting called specifically to exchange information on campus tensions and the fall semester outlook, the Associated Press quoted an unidentified top administrator of a large Midwestern university as saying: "I think it's clear to us that there are a bunch of pros at work, cynically manipulating our students. Compared to them we're a bunch of amateurs. If they want to shut us down, they can."

The candid admission that the universities could be shut down was frightening. But manipulation by power of suggestion is almost unbeatable if those responding are unaware of the techniques.

Traditional and increasing targets for radical movements, campuses present both comparatively easy access to masses and the open-mindedness of the young. They also usually have one or more professors in residence who sincerely believe in one or more radical causes. They gladly espouse, if not promote, their cause. Academic freedom must continue to assure opportunities to air any cause, far left or far right. However, to maintain that freedom, on campus or off, students and faculty may now have to learn some hard facts about the science of suggestibility—its negative and explosive factors, at least. Nazi Germany is a lesson.

Appearing at an Eastern university in 1969, I was quickly made aware of a movement, being manipulated largely by an off-campus nonstudent group, that was gathering momentum toward violence. My estimated audience that evening would number about three thousand, and the administration warned that there might be an attempt to use the mass gathering for other purposes. In defense alone, I decided to discuss some of the negative factors of suggestibility and demonstrate the role of controllers. I think the point hit home. A number of the demonstrators were present but no attempt was made to take over the stage or the mike.

Coupled with the negative factors of suggestibility, it strongly appears that *all* people tend to lose some degree of responsibility in a mob, feeling that they can eventually put the blame on those around them. They become less a part of the decisive factors. Obviously the conditioners or controllers take advantage of this protective coloration.

Not long ago, a New York psychologist decided to conduct an experiment on individual response as compared to multiple response in an identical situation. He placed an ad offering a job and then used his office as a "lab." It contained several chairs and couches in addition to a secretary's desk. A focal point was an overhead vent, used for heating and air conditioning. At a precise moment, smoke was fed through the vent. When one applicant was present, he rose immediately to tell the secretary that there might be a fire in the building. When two applicants were present, it took a longer time for them to warn of possible danger. When five were present, none got up immediately. In fact, several pretended they didn't notice the smoke, taking on protective coloration.

Dr. Freud appears to have been correct when he noted that man has a sheeplike quality on occasion, seeming to respond as a herd when grouped together. Control is possible with the emergence of a leader. Had one person in the room with the smoking vent assumed leadership, the four others would no doubt have responded immediately, "Yes, I do see smoke."

In riot cause and control, Congress might do better spending a few dollars on a handful of books written in the 1880's and 1890's than appropriating massive expenditures for commissions and investigations after the fact. Dr. Boris Sidis, with his *Psychology of Suggestion*; Dr. Hippolite Bernheim, with *Suggestion Therapeutics*; Dr. E. W. Scripture of Yale University, with *Power of Direct Suggestion*; as well as Ivan Pavlov of Russia, Albert Moll of Germany, and Otto G. Wetterstrand of Sweden—all explored mass human reactions almost a hundred years ago, and the factors remain the same. They are more explosive today because there are more of us around, usually very prone to suggestion.

As a dominating force in our lives, suggestion won't go away, politically or otherwise. As advertising, based mainly on suggestibility and persuasion in all its visual and aural forms, we wake up with it and go to bed with it. As with all

125

communications it is open to devious uses, and furor several years back over "subliminal advertising" was warranted if only for the purpose of investigation.

The idea behind it was reprehensible. Flashing almost imperceptible designs or words on movie or TV screens to influence buyers was an unparalleled concept in deceit. The possibility that it might succeed, dominating millions silently, was almost too staggering to contemplate.

It was first tried in drive-in theaters, where the word "popcorn," fitting indeed, was projected subliminally. Some reports indicated that sales were increased. Then it was discovered that many of the theater operators had moved their vending machines into more prominent positions to take full advantage of this new low in friendly persuasion. Finally one operator raised the sensible question: Is the sales increase the result of subliminal huckstering or better position of the poppers? The latter was indicated.

New Jersey was the first state legislatively to ban subliminal advertising and then all the networks banned it, practicing another type of mass hysteria. After the initial outcry was over, psychologists looked into selling by flash perception. There was no concrete evidence that the customer bought because of the flash, if he even saw it.

Yet the Orwellian attempt remains as a clear warning against tinkering with public forms of communication for purposes of mass persuasion. Suggestibility also has its "1984" aspects in the hands of an expert.

[7]

The late Edgar Cayce, "the sleeping prophet," has now become somewhat of an American saint in the peripheral areas of ESP. It is a role that he probably did not envision, nor would have wanted. Some of his readings, meditations and comments have been fashioned into a multitude of books bearing such titles as *Edgar Cayce on Atlantis* and *Edgar Cayce on Jesus Christ*. They tend to diminish what appears to have been a remarkable and unusual display of psychic power.

Except for Edgar Cayce, I have not been able to accept much "clairvoyance." But there is every indication that he had a gift, or developed some unusual technique, that could be applied to medical diagnosis. The talent, or whatever it was, is now known as "traveling clairvoyance."

At set times Cayce, in Virginia Beach, or wherever he happened to be, concentrated on diagnosing a patient's illness in a distant place. Thus far his "hits" have defied explanation. They have been probed from every possible angle by both medical and psychical researchers. Nothing conclusive, pro or con, has ever been established.

The problem with an Edgar Cayce, rare in any century, is that his success in healing encourages others who do not have similar gifts. The door is opened to those who plan fraud as well as to those who honestly believe they have "hidden" healing powers. For the victim, there is little difference between the quack and the well-intentioned friend who has achieved an *alpha* state as the result of a four-day course in mind control. Advertised in many major newspapers and magazines, the courses promise a greater control over emotions, a greater ability to relax, a greater potential for achievement and general all-round greater happiness, all sterling goals. A few advertisements claim that "abilities to practice ESP can be achieved," and that if one stays for the full four days, abilities to achieve the alpha state, or some other state, are said to be possible. One such course, disastrously, even hints that "medical diagnosis" is possible in such a state.

Recently, after a concert in Texas, I had dinner with the sponsor group. One attractive, apparently intelligent guest said that she had taken a mind control course; had achieved the alpha state and was now convinced that she had diagnostic capabilities. She said she had diagnosed stomach cancer in a friend and was now practicing "mental medicine." Had she told the friend of the exact diagnosis? Well, no. She didn't want to upset the lady. Besides, the patient seemed to be improving. My remark that both parties were suffering from a "dangerous delusion" brought about wild anger.

Some two years ago I enrolled one of my own friends into a mind-control class in New York City simply to monitor it. I was dying to know what went on. One of the first class exercises was to unite in a single thought to end the Vietnam war. A second exercise was to unite in a thought to save the life of a boy who was in a terminal condition at a Manhattan hospital. Three months later, with the Vietnam war still raging, and the boy dead, I had my monitor call the group leader for an explanation. The answer was, "God did not feel the time was right." God had to take the blame. However, my friend did report that he thought he had achieved the alpha state.

You can achieve the so-called alpha state, which is a difference in brain-wave patterns on the EEG, while reading this book. All you have to do is lift your eyes, daydream; just relax and daydream; let your eyes go out of focus, drift and daydream—float off mentally.

If you have an EEG handy, there'll be an alpha response on it.

Even as a layman, I do not see how the alpha state, which somehow ends up smacking of a "trance," can contribute to diagnosing a bunion. It goes back to Mesmer's day: A patient would be paraded in front of a "hypnotized good subject" who was said to be practicing "lucidity." The subject would then diagnose the patient's illness, sometimes prescribe medicine. The patient, of course, paid for such psychic deliverance. Very possibly, he also died.

There are several good "mind" courses but they stay well away from diagnosing ailments. Within the limitation of a few days, they are as beneficial and as acceptable as the Dale Carnegie courses. Depending on the individual they can, and do, increase an ability to relax and exert greater control over the emotions. They are largely in the "think positively" category, thanks to Émile Coué and his "Day by day in every way I am getting better and better."

A step beyond and yet a step back is *psychic surgery.* It comes full circle to the ancient "faith healers," even to Mesmer's belief that electrical energy healed. It is the possibility of healing through "fingertip" energy, with or without religious aspects.

Already Russian scientists, breaking ground again, claim to have recorded a strange energy force between mother and child. Further, photographs of a "mysterious corona" in the fingertips of certain faith healers, taken by the Kirlian process, with film exposed by pulsed electrical charges, indicate that additional research is worthwhile. But no area of psychic phenomena, no matter how ridiculous it seems, should remain unexplored.

Experimental work is being done in several clinics to "think heat and warmth" into the hands. Subjects sit with eyes closed and imagine that warmth is passing into their hands. A slight rise in the temperature of the hands has been noted in suggestible subjects. No one knows where it will lead, but it might be of minor aid in circulatory problems.

An offshoot of this work is the possibility of some relief of migraine headaches. An application, or "laying on," of warm hands to the head of the subject has appeared to alleviate migraine pain in some experiments. Perhaps a form of indirect suggestion takes place, causing a change in pressure on veins and arteries. So, imagination may be able to play a role in something as common and frustrating as the migraine. Though experiments of this sort must fall into the "far-out" category, in terms of what is known about psychology, it is alone significant that Stanford University is delving into psychic surgery.

Suggestion may also play a role in acupuncture, a treatment every bit as controversial as psychic surgery or faith healing. Prior to a treatment, Chinese doctors often lecture the patient, showing charts of the acupuncture points. This is followed by the procedure known as moxibustion, the rubbing of heated herbs into the flesh in the areas to be treated. The herbs have the odor of incense. These factors are suggestible in the conditioning sense.

Due to interest in acupuncture, and having a half-formed theory about the part that suggestion might play in the treatment, I invited an expert to appear on my television program. We discussed the procedures and then the expert pushed a needle into the fleshy part of my announcer's hand, between the thumb and the forefinger. Bill Luxton said that he "felt no pain."

Four audience volunteers, all middle-aged or over, had been requested to remain outside the studio during the discussion and needle demonstration. I then brought them inside, seating them on the stage, side by side. After a few minutes of explanation, I took an acupuncture needle and tapped the left hand and wrist of each subject. I did not penetrate the skin but tapped with enough force to have caused a reaction in an unconditioned person. They were aware of a sensation but felt no pain. The suggestion was through the needle. Their response blocked the needlepoint.

Next, I requested all four subjects to close their eyes so that they could not see which hand I would touch. I pinched the right hand of the first man very hard. He winced. The same reaction was achieved in the lady sitting next to him. Through suggestion, and the coupling of imagination, they had desensitized their left hands without the use of acupuncture.

Acupuncture is apparently much more than suggestibility but there appears to be a linkage of the two, and that linkage warrants investigation.

Healing will always be the most dynamic as well as the most dangerous single area of psychic phenomena. Despite tons of research, the emotions, and exactly how and when they interlock with the physical, are frustrating riddles. They play a part in many familiar incidents that occur far from the uncomfortable corridors of faith healing or acupuncture.

Liberace once approached a woman in his audience who had

been paralyzed and lame most of her life. He touched her. Promptly, she got up and walked. It was hardly faith healing. That elegantly dressed entertainer was as astounded as the lucky lady. Emotionally triggered autosuggestion? Who knows?

Putting on a performance of radio's *Truth or Consequences* in a service hospital, Ralph Edwards was told of a man who couldn't walk, though there was no apparent cause. Switching the format, Edwards brought in people from the man's past. At show's end, after giving the patient a charm bracelet, with all his friends and relatives gathered around, Edwards, at the suggestion of a psychiatrist, said, "Now, sir, here is your car, and the keys to it. Come over and get them." The patient shook, paused, rose up and walked across the stage. Emotionally triggered suggestibility? Perhaps. Out of this incident a very emotional show was born—Edwards' *This Is Your Life.*

Vivid in my own memory is an evening at a private party about six years ago. I had seated eight subjects in chairs and had told them that they would soon be leaving on a train trip and that they would describe the countryside and the towns they passed through as the train rolled along. I said I would give them a signal—they'd wave good-bye to relatives, and then the train would start. We did not take that imaginary trip. On my signal to depart, a young girl raised her arm to wave good-bye and there was an immediate outcry from many of the other guests in the room who were observing. The girl had not been able to lift her arm for three or four years because of a previous injury. Physical and psychiatric therapy eventually restored full use of the arm.

It appears that reactions in all of these cases were completely automatic. None of the patients were considering their affirmities at the moment. *Suggestion* went its own course.

[8]

It is probable that many people, with a limited concentration span, can never achieve telepathy, although the basic equipment is there. Thought perception takes years of sensitizing. Few people are inclined to spend the time and effort.

However, the use of suggestibility, as an extension of our normal use of suggestion, is possible for almost everyone. Salesmen employ it daily but few realize the total potential. Of course, to bring it to the refined state approaching the *science of suggestology* would also require years of effort.

But autosuggestion, as I practice it, is within easy reach of every human. With relatively little training and effort, it can be used in countless ways. No mind-control course is necessary, not even a "how to" book. Simplicity, not in the process but in utilization, is its chief asset. After a point it becomes as natural as sleeping and eating.

In one respect, autosuggestion is the absolute antithesis of the scientific method, which is to believe only what is observable, or based on past observations and explainable only according to scientific data. Admittedly, autosuggestion is also contrary to common-sense dictates. Despite science and the rules of common sense, it works.

As mentioned before, the key to the successful use of autosuggestion is one word—conviction. An old hymn says: "All things are possible, only believe." Another says: "Faith is victory." All things are not possible and faith isn't always victory, but in this case, ridiculous as it may sound, the conviction key carries more weight than science.

Conditioning is necessary. Call it *autoconditioning* or anything you choose. It is composed of a series of mental exercises that lead to the use of autosuggestion. However, they come in the usually palatable form of relaxation. In this game, as in most games, there are a few loose rules:

1. Make up your mind that you are *not* going to concentrate intently on the exercises while you practice them. If you do, how can you relax?

2. Be passive. Melt mentally. The imagination must be given a free rein. The unconscious functions independently of the conscious, so what may seem irrational is not. Suggestion and imagination work hand in hand again, so the widest mental plain should be opened.

With these two general guides in mind, the sequence for autoconditioning may be roughly patterned as follows:

1. Sitting in a deep chair, or lying down, make yourself comfortable.

2. Reflect for a few seconds on an experience in which you have achieved extreme relaxation—perhaps while spending a quiet afternoon on the beach, or falling asleep in front of a fireplace after a walk in the snow, or lying in deep shade on a riverbank. Recall as much of the experience as you can.

3. Close your eyes and think of your favorite passive color. Blues and greens work best for me.

4. After a few seconds, take three deep breaths. Hold the third, the deepest, and mentally repeat the color three times.

5. Exhale and go limp. Make no effort to move a muscle. Simply stay relaxed and count backwards, mentally from fifty to zero; *very slowly*. At zero, count forward from one to three. Open your eyes.

And that routine, consuming all of five minutes, is the first step (in my home-grown method) toward autoconditioning, which, in turn, sets the stage for successful autosuggestion. There are other ways to go about it, but I prefer the simplest route.

After doing it several times, you may find you lose track of numbers or perhaps skip a few. It doesn't matter. You'll end up on zero, which is the conditioning goal for relaxation.

During the first two weeks, practice three times daily, preferably at different periods of the day. It means closing off the world around for fifteen minutes, a time period which even the most harried mother and housewife or busiest executive should be able to afford.

Beginning with the third week, the sessions can be reduced to twice daily, but should not drop below that quota. Many people who have tried it prefer to maintain three a day, finding the experience pleasant rather than boring.

If miracles are not expected, if you don't question what is occurring and allow nature to take its course, you'll find you are increasing a level of general relaxation affecting both the muscles and nervous system, at the same time setting up conditions for autosuggestion to succeed.

Basically, it is accomplished by *not trying to relax* but by permitting the body and mind to take advantage of submission set up through the conditioned mind.

Relaxation can be learned, and even for the hyperactive individual it should not be overly difficult. Most experts on the subject concentrate on reducing body tensions. Once the body is relaxed, they maintain, the mind usually slacks off, too. The procedures are reversible, of course.

If you find that the easiest path to relaxation does not lead directly from the mind, then you approach it physically:

1. Sitting or lying down, immediately tense all muscles. Now relax and let go each set of muscles. Let your right arm go limp; then the left arm. Your right leg, then the left. Drop the shoulders, the back, the trunk. Even the eyelids are capable of reacting to a signal to relax.

2. As you initially relax each arm and leg, you'll find that other muscles are relaxing sympathetically. It is difficult to let go the tension in one arm and not have a response in the other. We return to the theory of the "whole" being; each member of the body is part of the whole body.

This sympathetic reaction of the muscles also illustrates how an attitude held in thought tends to affect the whole system. It is impossible to relax the body without a similar reaction in the conscious mind.

With this reverse course of conditioning now accomplished, and in only a few seconds, you can go back to the steps of thinking of a relaxing experience, a passive color, and the counting, from fifty back to zero.

Gradually, using either method, the process of conditioning can become such an integral part of your daily mental and physical nourishment that you'll find it a fortification against tension at home or in the office.

In time, the progressive relaxation can be dropped and instant relaxation can be achieved through mind control. The mind will do its job, on signal, responding in a few seconds. I've taught several beleaguered, harried TV announcers how to "come off it" in less than thirty seconds.

In the grind of today's world, this use of mind control for the purpose of relaxation alone would seem worthwhile. Fortunately, theory is not involved. Biofeedback researchers have established, through electrodes attached to subjects, that certain thought patterns can lower metabolism. Naturally, they can also increase it. Individuals who become skilled in the use of autoconditioning can relax while running or walking simply by feeding thoughts that work for them.

Conditioning having been achieved, the mind readied to receive and accept its singular important message, cleared of trivia and turmoil, the processes of autosuggestion are possible. Within these processes I have a theory that the unconscious is alerted and readied to become the holding place, perhaps the ultimate guiding place, for the thought.

The signal, or thought, can be something as simple as arousing promptly at 3 A.M. without use of an alarm, instant sleep on an aircraft, or the need to imbed a key answer to a troublesome exam question; an act of self-improvement, combating a habit or alleviating pain. I have used all of these, and many more, at one time or another. The limit is within the individual.

Pre-sleep autosuggestion can be a normal extension of its use, providing longer and deeper rest. We often take worries and problems to bed with us. As negatives, they forecast a restless, tossing night and possibly disturbing dreams. While total erasure may be impossible through autosuggestion, positive aspects can be implanted and will aid in sleep, and facing the new day with the same old problem will be easier.

Studies at the Maimonides Medical Center's Dream Laboratory have proven conclusively what had long been suspected— the sleeping period is far from dormant. During certain periods, the mind remains active and awake. There are also indications that it attempts to recuperate, and dreams are frequently important escape valves for accumulated pressures.

People are thought to be especially responsive to ideas and suggestions during the earlier periods of sleep, estimated at the first half-hour in the average person. This period, then, is the ideal time for the mind to receive and integrate constructive and acceptable suggestion.

The value of sleep-learning by recorded messages is, at best, woefully limited. It is likely that any learning process would have to take place during the early period, and there is no gauge as to the depth of the impression, if any takes place at all. In truth, the best response, in my experience, is the technique of introducing suggestions prior to falling asleep.

My method of pre-sleep conditioning goes back to Coué, stressing the positive. It doesn't need to be his exact famed slogan, but it should build self-esteem and look to a brighter personal tomorrow.

Although it may sound as if you're indulging in ego-polishing horseplay, assume your favorite sleeping position and mentally repeat "Autosuggestion is becoming the key to my daily self-improvement" or some variation. Even better is to create your own personal slogan, using vivid references. The slogan should be repeated twenty times. Move your lips as if you were speaking it aloud. Simultaneously, count on your fingers. Press each one against the thumb as the suggestion is repeated silently. Without realizing it, you're practicing both a mental and physical exercise. If you need to make it sound important, it's known as a *psychophysical* exercise.

The sequence should always be completed the first seven nights. After the first week or so, dozing off before completion will not disturb the pattern. Your lips will move and your fingers will press, carrying over into the doze.

Feed-in of the pre-sleep autosuggestion—whether it is to set a "timing device" in your mind to awaken at 6:30 A.M. or to probe the unconscious for a lost bank statement—is then coupled with the conditioning prior to the point of drifting off. "Where is that bank statement?"

Is it necessary to go through such a seemingly absurd routine, one so foreign to the average intellect? In most cases, I think it is. I think that the mind needs to be primed much as a carburetor primes an engine. I'm at a loss to know why some people reject the idea of intermental communication.

Practicing the simple arousal routine often, depending on it to catch the next jet for a play date, I've often wondered whether or not my unconscious literally "views" the clock at the appointed hour or whether it counts down from the time I went to sleep. How does it precisely awaken me at a specific time? I don't think that anyone knows.

Once again, the suggestion is quite temporary. It wears off in a few minutes to a dozen hours, and in the case of self-improvement, such as a golf game, must be reinforced constantly.

In cigarette smoking, the person who quits after one session of "hypnosis" or suggestion is primed to quit. He wants to quit and only needs a push. He must then carry on his own treatment by autosuggestion.

In achievement in job or career, autosuggestion is a reinforcement toward the aim. The aim is held in the mind and the signal is reinforced daily. In this instance, it reverts back to Peale's "power of positive thinking."

I remember sitting for an interview with news reporter Taylor Holbrook in the Schaefer House dining room, Phillipsburg, New Jersey, in 1966. Holbrook, of the Phillipsburg *Free Press*, had forgotten his notebook. Laughing, he said, "Why don't you hypnotize me, make me remember everything." I went through a systematic technique employing suggestion, and reinforced him several times during the two-hour conversation. Later, from total recall, he wrote a story of about a thousand words. However, it was his own mechanism, his acceptance of the fact that he would "remember everything," that enabled him to retain the details. His response indicated he might have accomplished the same thing through autosuggestion, reinforcing himself.

It is impossible to begin to cover the range of autosuggestion usage. In Russian experiments it is applied to cosmonauts to distort time. Through visual imagery occupying the mind, it can shorten time within the space capsule. An ordinary example of this is possible during any flight. Stare out of the window at cloud formations and think of something entirely removed from the aircraft. See it mentally, savor it. Ten minutes can become one.

Golf has a peculiar problem, I believe. Unlike basketball or football, the player can become too self-indulgent between holes. He competes with himself as well as with the other players. He has time between shots to reflect on the mistakes of the last hole and worry about the next one. There is ample time to feed in negative information which may well affect his play. With autosuggestion, he can deflect the negative and turn it positive.

Although the removal of pain by autosuggestion is a myth, as it is by "hypnosis," it can be somewhat deadened or divided. It can be made to feel "detached." If imagination can convert a mere touch of the finger into a shooting pain, as has been proven by suggestibility, then this same mental tool can be employed, in some circumstances, to alleviate severe agony. It cannot remove it, and the time span is limited.

I think the dangers of the use of autosuggestion for pain alleviation are exaggerated. Some psychiatrists claim that autosuggestion may have lasting negative effects because a pain is being masked. This falls into the category of a thousand different psychological "may have's." So far, there is no factual support to indicate that a person who uses his mind to alleviate pain, *something the human species has probably been doing since creation*, will suffer later mental damage. However, he may delay needed medical attention.

The real danger in autosuggestion, in my opinion, is that people will expect results, in any given situation, beyond its capability.

[9]

The first definitive American work on "hypnosis" was written by Dr. George H. Estabrooks, professor of psychology at Colgate University. Titled *Hypnotism*, it was published in 1943. Though it was my scientific bible for years, I now consider it, and most other works in the same field, as science fiction. I arrived at that conclusion eight years ago after "hypnotizing" an estimated thirty-five thousand people.

For nineteen years I had believed in Estabrooks and the sleeplike "hypnotic trance," practicing it constantly. Though I had nagging doubts at times, I wanted to believe in it. There was an overpowering mystique about putting someone to sleep, something that set me and all other "hypnotists" apart. We were marvelous Svengalis or Dr. Mesmers, engaged in a supernatural practice of sorts. Then it all collapsed. For me, anyway.

The Svengalian phenomenon has quite a history. A number of European medical doctors and journalists believed that

Austrian physician Franz, or Friedrich, Anton Mesmer (1733–1815) was nothing but a dangerous fraud; others eventually claimed he was the true father of "hypnosis." Events have proved he probably doesn't deserve either lot.

Ultimately chased out of both Vienna and Paris for his supposedly crackpot theories, Dr. Mesmer's discovery and downfall began when he became fascinated with magnets and experimented by holding them over his patients. Some, he discovered, reacted by shaking or having spasms, then appeared to be cured of their illnesses or manifestations of illness. For a time he was convinced that the lodestone electrical force was a curative.

His fascination is understandable. Medicine was still relatively primitive in the eighteenth century and the magnet was one of the most mysterious objects on earth. Well before Mesmer, Catholic Father Maximilian Hell, who has been lost in the history of "hypnotism," toyed with magnets.

Mesmer had begun healing with them in Vienna, but his clientele was mostly limited to the wealthy and bored. That circumstance often seems to have crawled over to today's psychoanalysis couch. However, the élite took interest in his work and spread the word. Mozart, for one, commented on it after Mesmer helped a "blind" pianist regain her sight. As frequently occurs, the psychological cure had its penalty: Mesmer lost favor with Maria Theresa's family because the pianist's income went down when she was no longer "blind." There was no audience sympathy.

After further experimentation, Mesmer decided that perhaps his own magnetism, and not the iron he was holding, was responsible for healing. He then began to theorize on animal magnetism: *that certain human beings could exert a magnetic or force influence over others; that it could drain out illness or other negative factors.* Psychic surgery?

In 1766 Mesmer wrote a book entitled *De planetarum influxu,* now a collector's item avidly studied by students of psychic medicine, on how the stars and planets influence human beings. Adopting some theories of the oldest occult belief, astrology, he quickly gathered a following.

In practice, Mesmer and his disciples, termed "magnetists" by that time, treated patients with stroking gestures, discarding the magnet, causing energy to flow from their fingertips. It was current-day faith healing without religious aspects. The patient did not go limp when the treatment supposedly took effect. They went into fits. Eyes closed, they shook all over, screamed, fell on the floor, banged their heads violently, then went limp, perhaps from exhaustion. Mesmer called this the "crisis," believing that it was a necessary factor in effecting the cure.

How his theory evolved is not known, but there is suspicion that a lot of his patients in Vienna were narcissistic, self-indulgent hypochondriacs. Their problems might have resulted more from boredom than from anything else. Releasing tension with loud screams and writhing was a cure of sorts.

As the story goes, one of his most learned disciples was the Marquis de Puységur, who lived in the bucolic village of Buzancy near Soissons, France. Enter a peasant boy in his teens named Victor Race. He suffered from violent headaches and was told to go to the local "magnetist," or "mesmerist,"— the marquis. Now, Victor had never seen a demonstration of "mesmerism" and had no idea that he was supposed to throw a fit before he was cured.

He sat down in the traditional way and the marquis began his flowing gestures which started at Victor's forehead and continued down to his feet. Victor apparently didn't know what to make of this, but his eyes did close and soon his head nodded.

The marquis waited. No tremor, no screaming. He was puzzled but finally asked, in essence, "Are you all right? Can you hear me?"

Obviously very relaxed, Victor reportedly answered in a faraway voice, taking on a role, "Yes."

The marquis then said a few other things and the boy answered. He was asked to move his arm. After a pause Victor moved his arm in a lethargic way. Soon the marquis discovered that whatever the boy was told, he did. He moved, talked and responded to *suggestion.* He looked to be "asleep" and therefore the marquis decided he was in a "trance."

At the end of the session the marquis made gestures in the opposite direction, upward, as usual, to "de-mesmerize" the patient, throwing away the invisible now-spent "magnetic fluid." He finally got the boy to open his eyes and asked how he felt. Victor responded that he felt fine but had difficulty in remembering what had happened.

The marquis, convinced that he had discovered a new psychic state, didn't know what to call it. Eventually he settled for "somnambulism," sleepwalking, derived from the Latin words *somnus,* "sleep," and *ambulare,* "walk."

Medical writers and psychologists interested in the field have pinpointed the Marquis de Puységur incident as the first formal discovery of "hypnosis," growing out of Mesmer's earlier experiments. In truth, Victor was responding in a different manner to the same old modality—suggestion. More important, if the story is true as we know it the boy knew nothing about "mesmerism" or what to expect, or how he was supposed to act. But apparently he was *suggestible,* and here was a man making gestures over him, not too far removed from a mother stroking a child's head to console. He relaxed.

Downward passes of the hand tend to cause blinks. In his case it could have been misinterpreted as an instruction to close his eyes. From his point of view, something was certainly expected. The easiest and simplest reaction was to close his eyes. But aside from the absence of screaming and writhing, there was really nothing different in this session and prior "magnetist" sessions. Both ended limp. Victor just didn't have to go through the preconditioning of a self-induced fit. Within twenty years, mesmerism shed its staged fits.

There were occasional exceptions and they still occur. A subject who is inclined to be hysterical, particularly one with exhibitionist tendencies, will scream during a *suggested* state.

Early Sinatra and Elvis Presley and later the Beatles created much the same phenomenon, including fainting, without magnets or "hypnosis."

Notable is the fact that most of Mesmer's "séances," as he called them—not in the spirit sense but in group participation —had interaction between people, today's group therapy. Of course, some of the same interaction was evident in Sinatra's appearances in the forties. Aided by drugs or not, it applies to present rock concerts. "Sent" and "far out" are not idle terms.

Not surprisingly, Mesmer was hounded. Medical concern in both Vienna and Paris, aimed at eliminating quackery, was the principal cause. A lesser reason was that Dr. Mesmer was getting both attention and patients. Traditional vested medical interests have always moaned at the mention of psychic healing.

Even Benjamin Franklin found himself involved in the Mesmer controversy. In France to request aid for the new American states in 1784, he was asked to judge mesmerism as part of a commission. In a separate opinion, Franklin said there was no proof of a special "mesmeric ability" and that the "claims of mesmerism for lucidity were unfounded." Then Franklin made a devastating remark, for that time: ". . . the response of the subjects was imagination."

What Dr. Mesmer had really found, in my opinion, was not "hypnosis" but *suggestive response,* the climate of triggered sensitivity that has always existed in man. He groped, and with the marquis, put his finger near the trigger, unknowingly making a valuable contribution.

Despite the rude treatment of Mesmer, France soon became the center of medical "hypnosis." Jean Martin Charcot, Pierre Janet, Hippolite Bernheim, Bertrand, A. A. Liebeault and La Fontaine all explored it with varying results.

Freud, becoming interested after witnessing demonstrations by a Danish entertainer named Hansen, attended the lectures of Dr. Charcot, Europe's leading psychiatrist in the 1850's. Charcot had decided that only hysterical people could be "hypnotized," mainly the mentally ill, and often lectured at Salpêtrière, using the mental institution in Paris as a laboratory. He was the first prominent psychiatrist, but not the last, to go completely astray in the field. His voluminous writings on the subject of medical "hypnosis" have largely been discredited.

A vain, Napoleonic figure, Charcot never personally "hypnotized" any subject, which was a great mistake. He employed several assistants to achieve the state. They worked constantly with about six subjects, all women. Both laymen and doctors attended the demonstrations as if they were freak shows. Even the most disreputable stage "hypnotist" would have considered Charcot's routine disgraceful and demeaning.

After he died, the same subjects he used for medical experimentation would put on a Sunday afternoon show at Salpêtrière without being "hypnotized." For a few coins, with no aid from Charcot's assistants, they would exhibit pain endurance, stretch themselves between two chairs and exhibit other familiar routines. They were not quite as "mad" as Charcot had estimated.

In contrast, retiring Hippolite Bernheim was pointing out that the true "hypnotic" response usually occurred in normal people, or the relatively normal—that it was, in fact, *suggestion.* Dr. Bernheim was the first to say publicly that the "hypnotic sleep trance" did not exist. He wrote an unpopular paper on the subject and it is still treated as contaminated pulp in many quarters.

But the man who contributed the term, a Britisher, Dr. James Braid, began as a disbeliever. He attended a performance of La Fontaine's. At first Braid called La Fontaine a fraud but changed his mind after a series of demonstrations. He then invented the term "neurohypnotism," later shortened to "hypnotism," from the word Hypnos, the Greek god of sleep, brother of Thanatos, death.

Near the end of his life, Braid began to understand more about the phenomenon and attempted to change the word to "mono-ideism," meaning "one thought." However, Braid was stuck with "hypnosis," and so are we. In fact and fiction, in medicine and in entertainment, it will likely be forever identified as a state of sleep. At best, it is a very false and needless sleep.

France made a contribution toward the truth through Coué, who was billed by press agents as a psychotherapist but in actuality was a pharmacist who had become interested in "hypnosis." After creating a stir in Europe, Coué came to America in 1920 preaching but one thing, his "better and better in every way."

Although he was an expert in "hypnotism," Coué eventually shunned it. Instead, his efforts were toward self-improvement by *suggestion* without the drag of a trance state. Oversold by publicity and finally discredited, his preachment ended up as passing fancy. Despite the somewhat silly-sounding bromide, Coué was on the right track. And his bromide, now employed in autosuggestion, is not as silly as it sounds. Self-esteem is recognized as the single most important item in mental health.

Although Bernheim, Janet and Braid, among others, gave "hypnosis" a feeble recognition as something more than "mesmerism," it has always been under a cloud, either feared or jeered. For more than a hundred years it has been the butt of "evil eye" jokes and cartoons. What could be worse for its image than to have men like Rasputin, Count Cagliostro and Adolf Hitler practice it? It's remarkable that no "hypnotist," of record, has ever been burned at the stake.

Yet, even in vaudeville days, probably the lowest point of respectability, there were legitimate and responsible stage "hypnotists" doing two-hour concerts and actually "hypnotizing." In contrast, the performers who had twelve-minute segments on the circuits used "horses," assistants who traveled with them from town to town. They rejected local volunteers as being "unhypnotizable," and beckoned their "horses" up. Little wonder that it was labeled phony.

145

[10]

There are many methods of inducing "hypnosis," and in the comic strips even cats have now found their methods for "hypnotizing" mice. The Svengali-Trilby relationship is endless. The "hypnotist" says, "Look at something on the wall." It can also be a candle flame, watch fob, key ring, or a marble on the table. The object is usually small. As a fixed object, a mountain obviously presents difficulties in narrowing attention.

Then: "Your eyes are getting heavy. So heavy. So very heavy. They can't be kept open. You're blinking. Your arms are getting heavy. Your legs are getting heavy. You're becoming drowsier . . . and drowsier . . . and drowsier . . . you want to sleep . . ."

The subject is literally *conned* into what the "hypnotist" thinks is a "trance." He has boxed this mind, separated it for his own control. He believes the subject is in a state where he is completely unaware of his own existence within the body.

After all these years, many "hypnotists" still do not realize that it is very difficult for most people to stare fixedly. The natural tendency is for the subject to blink. He "waters" his eyes for lubrication. But when the subject hears the "hypnotist" say, "Your eyes are blinking," he thinks, "The 'hypnotist' is right. My eyes are blinking. I am responding. It's working!"

At that precise moment he is emotionally involved. He is beginning to believe that he can and will respond. He has been sitting still, and development of "sensory awareness" has begun. The arm that can itch so easily with no "hypnotist" within ten miles can also become "heavy" simply by suggestion.

Then the curtain opens on the playlet between the "hypnotist" and the slumped-over, "entranced" subject. In this psychodrama, there is considerable action on the part of both performers.

I slowly realized that the possibility existed that the "sleep trance" was an invention passed along from Mesmer's days. I went back to Bernheim's writings and suddenly "hypnosis" began to reek. I now realize that as a teen-ager I submerged doubts while working with Anna Piukutowski. I had been told that when a good subject entered a deep trance, the "rapport" would be so strong that (1) the subject could not hear anyone except the "hypnotist," (2) the subject would ignore any directions and even the physical presence of outsiders. With Aunt Anna deep in an apparent trance, I would impress on an audience her complete separation by having people come up to say, "Aunt Anna, wake up." Each time I noticed that she would begin to stir, moving her head. I'd quickly end the test. Obviously, I was afraid she would awaken, and also afraid to admit she could hear other voices. Plainly, she was never "asleep."

Twenty years having passed, I decided to use my stage shows as an experimental laboratory. In the second half of the program, prior to "hypnotizing" anyone, I tried to induce them to do the same things without setting up a "trance." There would be no "sleep," no slumped-over posture.

At first, possibly because I wasn't certain that it could be done, I had many failures. But as the months went by, I began to improve on my techniques. As a showman, I had learned how to get attention and the trust of my audience, a prerequisite for accomplishing anything by "suggestion." It is also one explanation why medical "hypnosis" has never been very productive. Very few doctors are skilled at it and are unable to work with it constantly.

With audience volunteers, complete strangers, I edged into it by first attempting to read their thoughts. This was mainly a crutch for me, and had little to do with their later response. After that, I finally succeeded in doing everything previously labeled "hypnotic" by simply getting their attention: freezing, at my suggestion, in an awkward position; seeing things that weren't there; imitating well-known entertainers; finding their hands spinning, one around the other. It took two years to perfect.

Throughout it all, I kept going back to the nonscientific, "nonhypnotic" example of Ralph Edwards. Through audience interaction and encouragement, and a form of suggestibility, he had achieved almost the same things in the television version of *Truth or Consequences*. He had people doing the wildest things without the slightest mumbo-jumbo or dangling watches or saying, "You're getting drowsier and drowsier . . ." He enticed them, motivated them, and "paid" them, in terms of awards.

There was a solid basis, I believed, on which to question the "sleep trance," which has always been the chief manifestation of "hypnosis." And as much as anything, it has been the spooky, mystical state which has foundered the true "hypnotic phenomenon," whatever it is, on the rocks of the occult and other nonsense. I decided that if modern science had not been able to understand the phenomenon in more than two hundred years, explain how or why it really works, then it was open to many questions.

I'm now convinced that no person under "hypnosis" has ever been asleep unless sent to that nontrance happy state by the lullaby drone of the guide. I am convinced that there is no such thing as a specific state, condition, trance—call it anything with any twist of semantics—that can be considered "hypnosis."

Brain-wave patterns on the electroencephalograph will show that a person supposedly in a "deep trance state" produces exactly the same patterns as if he were totally awake. A polygraph test will prove that the subject is aware of everything that goes on. Therefore, he cannot be *asleep*, unless the definition of sleep is changed.

Simply to make it worthwhile as a scientific endeavor, pay for time involved, I've offered twenty-five thousand dollars to anyone who can prove, conclusively, the existence of the "hypnotic trance." Over a period of three years, my challenge has been accepted on three occasions but abandoned each time. The EEG and polygraph are formidable opponents.

One by one each manifestation of so-called "hypnosis" has been discredited:

(1) The sleep trance has been discredited.

(2) The unconscious state has been discredited.

(3) Regression has been discredited.

(4) The hysterical state has been discredited.

(5) The conditioned-reflex state has been discredited.

If all these theories have been discarded by reputable authorities, dating back to Dr. Braid, we are left with the dilemma of trying to define a supposedly abnormal state or condition without a scientific barometer to make positive judgment. What causes us to respond to suggestion cannot be readily explained. Therefore, it must be called "hypnosis." Otherwise, it poses a threat to our reasoning.

The battle of semantics may be waged for years, but I firmly believe that what is termed "hypnosis" is, again, a completely normal, not abnormal, response to simple suggestion. But for many reasons, not the least financial, it will be mystically mined for a long time to come.

At the risk of being passed off as an idiot entertainer who has reached a true state of psychosis, I believe that research scientists in "hypnosis" have continually made one colossal mistake—that of not being strictly scientific. Their controlled laboratory experiments, often with the same people, "good subjects," bring about predictable results. A commonly used estimate is that only one person out of every ten is a "good subject." The researcher is apt to use a "good subject" both to save time and to gain "deep" results.

Within the lab, there is little astounding about inducing a subject to feel "light" or "heavy" or imagine that he is in Haiti or on the moon. What is amazing is that most researchers have never gotten around to establishing the fact that the subject, in his "trance," knows that he isn't in Haiti or in a crater. More amazing, though, is the fact that all but a few medical "hypnosis" experts completely accept the "trance" state.

One scientist who has dismissed the "sleep trance" and "hypnosis" is Dr. Barber of the Medfield Institute. Supported partially by federal funds, Dr. Barber has made countless experiments and has written more than one hundred papers on the subject. His findings are often met with wailings and recriminations in the field because there is that usual dollar mark on "hypnosis." Entertainers, doctors, dentists, psychologists, writers and hypnotists of a dozen varieties make money from it.

Dr. Barber reached the firm conviction, far beyond Bernheim's position of long ago, that there is no evidence of any special condition of "trance" that we currently label "hypnosis," or anything slightly suggestive of it. In his lab he has demonstrated, as I've done onstage, that most normal people can be motivated and persuaded in a wide-awake state simply by applied *suggestion*.

What happens is more in the realm of Coué and of Peale's *Power of Positive Thinking* than in the freaky halls of Svengali. Everything is within the person. He does not need to assume an unnatural state to utilize mental capabilities whether for fun, relaxing tension, pain suppression or achieving greater potential. In addition, after all his extensive research Dr. Barber does not know "what makes a good hypnotic subject." Neither do I. Obviously some people are more susceptible than others to this psychic response, by any name. But the exact "why" remains unknown, except that imagination and creativity seem to help.

In our separate ways, both Dr. Barber and I have found that if a subject is *suggestible* and has the capacity to accept an idea, if he is properly motivated and willing, and if some scope of imagination is present, he can be persuaded to do every single thing that is currently done under the guise of entranced "hypnosis."

I'll use the oldest known example, which dates back to Dr.

Charcot, and perhaps to Mesmer: the rigidity state between two chairs. Long ago I bridged Johnny Carson between two chairs without use of "hypnosis." I use Carson as an example because, again, it was done in public, before cameras and a live audience. Wide awake, Carson functioned normally in every sense except that of muscular reaction.

Had it been "hypnosis," the performance on network TV would have been impossible due to restrictions brought about by a pair of concerned New York psychiatrists, Drs. Harold Rosen and Herbert Spiegel. They succeeded in abolishing examples of formal hypnosis from television, reportedly for fear of having the masses influenced.

At any rate, Carson was bridged between two chairs, head on one, feet on the other, with singer Bette Middler sitting on his stomach. Johnny knew where he was, who he was, and what he was doing. Tapes of the show will prove that he was talking throughout the demonstration without the faraway voice of a trance. He said there was "no strain at all."

As additional public proof, I've done it with Mike Douglas on his show; on my own show with actors Eddie Albert and Van Johnson; on the concert stage and in nightclubs with volunteers. They were wide awake. Admittedly, it is not accomplished with the method usually employed by the stage "hypnotist," the "become rigid, stiff, rigid, like a bar of steel" method. Estabrooks did it that way; I used the same technique for many years.

In the usual stage demonstration, someone can sit or stand on the subject's stomach, similar to the Carson test. But there is a possibility of strain because the subject is so engrossed in the "hypnotist," so intent on achieving the bridge that he is not aware of the strain. The muscles are locked. The "hypnotist" is the external influence, while in my method of pure *suggestion* the subject takes his own directions to cantilever his back, adjusting himself to the pressure comfortably. I've had as many as three sitters on the subject without any evidence of strain on his part, then or later. However, I wouldn't select a little old lady for the demonstration, although she'd undoubtedly be capable.

This type of presentation, always associated with "deep hypnosis or trance," brought about immediate allegations that Carson was "hypnotized" before the show went on the air and that I then gave him a "secondary suggestion." So far as I can recall, I only saw him for a minute, to reassure him that he'd suffer no physical harm, before going out to join his guests. Not unexpectedly, most of the accusing mail came from "hypnotists" and not from the general public.

I appreciate the fact that some medical doctors are alarmed at the prospect of an intrigued public attempting to bridge chairs as a result of a demonstration or indulge in "self-hypnosis" after seeing a TV show. The likelihood of either experiment succeeding is in the same ratio as shooting a hole in one after watching Arnold Palmer, and involves about the same hazard. As to the effects on children, I'd rather have them experiment with *suggestion* than watch most of TV's murder and mayhem.

The safety factor in "self-hypnosis" is that it doesn't work. No one has ever learned how to go into so-called "deep trance" after reading a how-to book. I'm a prime example. I've tried to "hypnotize" myself on hundreds of occasions. Nothing has ever happened. It has always bothered me that I could put thousands of people into "hypnosis" but not myself. I'm not alone. Harry Arons, a professional in the field, flatly states that "no one can learn self-hypnosis from a book."

My own belief, based on personal experience, is that when a subject is his own "hypnotizer," he knows he is not going to be entranced. The conscious may beckon him but reason tells him no real trance is occurring. He works at it, and waits, and waits. I have an idea he can wait until his hair grows white. No one is there to convince him or guide him. He eventually becomes disgusted, as I have many times, and talks himself out of even superficial response.

Though I'm now attempting to shatter the "sleep trance"

myth, I strongly believe that the phenomenon of "hypnotic" suggestibility has been overly maligned and made a goat for endless reasons. Use of the "horses" in earlier years, and even today; the fact that it is still shrouded in the unexplainable; and because it occasionally offers a seemingly handy explanation for irrational human behavior, all have contributed to a shadowy reputation.

Several years ago a book by Robert Kaiser entitled *RFK Must Die* theorized that Sirhan Sirhan assassinated Senator Robert Kennedy after being "hypnotically" programmed. Apparently this was the author's own premise. It received attention on television and in some magazines. I was asked to endorse it and perhaps appear in a film based on parts of the book. I declined. The premise was entirely false.

During the Sirhan Sirhan trial a physician, obviously trained in "hypnotic techniques," was brought in by the defense to testify that perhaps the alleged assassin had been "hypnotized" prior to the shooting because he went under "hypnosis" so easily. That leads into the "posthypnotic suggestion" area, of course. We then have a "Manchurian Candidate," which was bang-up fiction. So was Sirhan Sirhan's "hypnosis." Had the jury bought this theory, the future of felony defenses would have had to include a session with a "hypnotist," after which the criminal could shed all personal responsibility and blame it on his "trance." It was a neat ploy on the part of the defense, but it did not work.

In laboratories, where the "hypnotized" subject knows that the gun handed to him by the professor is loaded with a blank, hypothetical murder can be successful. So the professor theorizes that the subject will fire that gun under real conditions, as programmed. Every researcher I've talked to has admitted he has never tried it with a live bullet, for obvious reasons. This lab experiment therefore remains theory. So does the experiment with a vial of "acid" which is really water. The subject flings it but knows he is not tossing acid with criminal intent.

Rape while supposedly entranced is fantasy. Doctors and dentists who practice "hypnosis" wisely carry insurance against the possibility of a rape claim. But the woman who cries rape and blames it on "hypnosis" is either a fraud or a victim of her own imagination.

In the thousands of times that I was under the assumption I had "hypnotized" people, I cannot recall a single occasion when I was able to persuade a subject to do anything he or she did not want to do. And these were mainly harmless, silly requests. Even so, no subject complied, consciously or unconsciously, unless he was willing to do so.

On four occasions, after being challenged by one psychologist or another, I have attempted to test the theory of submission against the will. I took a butcher knife to a demonstration in Bloomfield, New Jersey, and made a choice of a young audience volunteer who had "gone under" rapidly. He appeared to be an excellent subject, and was responding easily to other tests. I told him that within five minutes after he awakened and took his seat in the audience, he would have an overwhelming urge to return to the stage. A butcher knife would be on the table and he was to plunge it into my back. I was confident that he would not do it; at the same time, there is always a chance that this much-doubted theory is correct. I admit to a slight uneasiness that day.

Five minutes later, as he left his seat and began to advance toward the stage, a dropped feather might have made a noise in the auditorium. It was not a lab setting, nor was the young man a repeated experimental subject. He had a preoccupied and detached look on his face as he reached the steps and I turned my back. Slanting slightly, so that I had peripheral vision to my left, I saw him pick up the butcher knife. He had some eight feet to go to reach me. When I saw him raise the knife I had a sudden desire to run. But then, about two feet away, he froze and I heard the knife hit the stage; I turned and saw revulsion on his face. His knees buckled a bit and I quickly reprogrammed him.

For the sake of both the demonstrator and the subject, it is not a type of experiment that should be attempted very often. My point in doing it out of a lab setting and with a subject off-the-streets was to substantiate the "alter" theory that it is not possible to program an act which is against the nature of the subject.

Yet I've considered several flaws which have nothing to do with the nature of the subject: he might believe that I had protected myself with a steel plate, or that the knife had a trick blade and wouldn't cut—that it was, in fact, one of the usual controlled lab experiments. Though remote, these circumstances are possible.

Eventually a question was posed involving one area of this test. Would it be possible to "stop" the subject by means of telepathy? I think so, and it's an experiment worthy of a try. Theoretically the act is against the subject's will, and any mental persuasion would reinforce that will.

More than theory is the lack of evidence of any murder being committed under "hypnosis." The classic case, one cited by some medical authorities as proof of "suggestive crime," involved a man named Hardrup. Even Estabrooks, in a recent reprint of his work, pointed to the Hardrup case as proof of entranced crime.

Hardrup was in a Copenhagen jail for a period in the mid-fifties. On release he robbed a bank and killed a bank official. After he was brought to trial, a Danish psychiatrist testified that Hardrup had been "hypnotized" by his cell mate, a man named Nilsson, and programmed to rob a bank—to kill, if necessary. Publications in the United States and other parts of the world picked this up and it snowballed into a flat fact. Articles and chapters in medical "hypnosis" books, and some criminology books, still chant it as gospel.

The court, however, discarded "hypnosis" as a factor. The jury was instructed to regard it as meaningless. The convict "hypnotist" was proved to have been involved in spiritualism and other occult attitudes. Games in this area were played in the cell. But "posthypnotic suggestion" had nothing to do, in the court's opinion, with the vicious act in the bank. The robber's cell mate might have suggested looting but the participant wasn't "triggered" by remote control, nor did he commit the act against his will. It isn't possible. Nature seems to have provided a safeguard against this.

Meanwhile the psychiatrist wrote a book devoted entirely to the crime, placing all the blame on "hypnosis." He failed to change the jury's decision, or later appeals, but managed to influence minds, including Estabrooks', on a world-wide basis by another type of suggestion—speculation.

Another well-known case took place in England in the early fifties. It involved an American stage "hypnotist," Ralph Slater, who was sued by a young lady he had previously mesmerized. The girl's expert witness was a medical "hypno-tist," Dr. Van Pelt, who had, it was later discovered, a personal ax to grind with Slater. Specifically, the girl accused Slater of "mental damages and harm" and won the suit. Van Pelt had treated her.

What is remarkable about the Slater case, in modern times and in England of all places, is that he was not permitted to face the jury lest he "hypnotize" them. Later the verdict was reversed and Slater was proved innocent of "mental damage." But as usual, the reversal received little attention and it went down in the books as further proof of the dangers of "hypnosis." England had passed legislation against the public practice of "hypnosis" as a result of the case but later relented, so the Svengalis can again practice their sleeping sessions in public.

"Hypnosis" was once more a psychical target when Dr. Herbert Spiegel, associate professor of psychiatry at Columbia University, presented the broadcasting industry with a test conducted before a medical audience. As previously mentioned, Dr. Spiegel is one of the two psychiatrists who can take large credit for the formal banning of "hypnotic" experiments from network TV.

Two people were brought into a room and were requested to sit before a TV set. Upstairs in another room Dr. Spiegel, introduced as a specialist in medical "hypnosis," looked into his camera and spoke to the subjects below, eventually putting them into a "trance." He ordered them to raise their hands, and then told one subject, a lady, that she could not lower hers. The gentleman, a salesman, was unable to release his clasped hands. These are routine, typical tests. They proved, it was claimed, "that people could be 'hypnotized' by watching a TV screen." Startling!

Later Dr. Spiegel came downstairs to release his subjects. The networks, rightfully alarmed at the possibility of home viewers being "hypnotized," reacted as expected. They banned further "hypnotic demonstrations."

Confident on the ground that I was on, I maintained that Spiegel's demonstration was misleading. I did not think that it was a legitimate medical experiment, done with complete strangers, normal composition of a home audience. To open it to public examination, and to re-examination by the network executives, I invited Dr. Spiegel to appear with me on the *Merv Griffin Show,* not only to debate it but to conduct a similar experiment under *uncontrolled* conditions, with as many audience volunteers as he desired. He ignored the invitation.

The element that disturbed me was the fact that Dr. Spiegel's subjects, the lady and the salesman, *were not innocent viewers* in their living rooms watching a "hypnotic" demonstration for the first time. The lady had been "hypnotized" several times before by Dr. Spiegel or his assistant. The other subject, so far as is known, had not been "hypnotized" previously by the psychiatrist, but then Spiegel's team mate admitted it had been determined that the salesman was "hypnotizable." To me, this means they had met the gentleman before, had talked to him, had determined that he could be "put under."

Additionally, what made the experiment somewhat questionable, from a professional standpoint, is the fact that both subjects were aware that they were participating in a test and being observed by a whole battery of medical men. A reaction was expected of them, and being readily "hypnotizable," they reacted. I believe that any good "hypnotist" could probably put the lady "under" with a phone call, without need for a TV monitor set.

Having been accused of playing a role in murder, rape, swindle, alienation of affections, and suspected by learned people of having the capacity to put a million video watchers into trance, the "hypnosis" phenomenon will probably never come out from under its own shadow. Some of its practitioners do not materially aid in the emergence. A few maintain that they can "hypnotize" certain animals and birds. They cite the rooster as proof. It is known that that barnyard fellow can be induced to stay motionless for a long time if you plunge his beak down to earth and focus his eyes on a long white line. I doubt that he's in a "trance." If the rooster is at all capable of thought, he's probably wondering what fool got him into that crazy position.

Some have said that the only way a snake charmer avoids a fang is through use of "hypnotism." Patient study has revealed that the cobra is fascinated by the movement of the charmer's body rather than the message in his eyes or entrancing fluting. And years ago I almost fell out of my chair while watching one of Steve Allen's TV shows that dealt with bird-and-beast entrancement. The featured guest was Dr. William J. Bryan, Jr., director of the now nineteen-year-old American Institute of Hypnosis, headquartered in Los Angeles. Dr. Bryan said that President Kennedy's Thanksgiving turkey might be more tender if it were "hypnotized" prior to the falling of the ax.

Perhaps it's healthier if "hypnosis" does remain under a shadow.

[11]

In 1958 the American Medical Association announced its official acceptance of "hypnosis" as a legitimate aid to the practice of healing. The AMA is conservative, and certainly should be where psychic phenomena are concerned, but the announcement came some two thousand years after the first recorded hints of suggested response, in any form, under any name.

In 1972, although public interest was higher than ever in the entire field of ESP, medical interest in "hypnosis" was predictably on the wane again. It peaked in 1958 with an estimated eight percent of the doctors and dentists showing some interest, a lesser number actually practicing it. Now practice involving "hypnosis" is estimated to be down to three percent and will probably sink lower.

Since Mesmer's day, there have been five distinct cycles of public interest in "hypnosis," with medical interest appearing to be largely a feedback from the public, the same stimuli now prodding ESP.

Although medical science will probably dispute it, I believe more knowledge about "hypnotism" has been unwittingly contributed over the years by the lowly stage "hypnotist" than by medical scientists. Proportionately, the medical experience is minute. Only a fragment of all people who have been truly and legitimately "hypnotized" have been entered into that state by doctors and dentists. The periodical medical disenchantment has usually come about through overselling.

It doesn't cure as forecast.

It remains questionable as an aid in psychiatric treatment.

It is not reliable as a pain suppressant.

It is not the answer to diet problems, nor to alcoholism or drug habits.

It has only succeeded, in a minor way, as a deterrent to smoking and improvement in physical skills.

Recently the aforementioned Dr. Bryan of the American Institute of Hypnosis claimed that a time would come when a football team's training schedule would call for a period on the "hypnotist's" couch. Further, he stated that a team physician could use "hypnotism" to set a player's broken leg or sprained limb almost immediately with practically no pain or swelling, and the recuperative time would be diminished. Dr. Bryan said this would be achieved "through subconscious control of the autonomic nervous system."

It has never lived up to such claims and never will.

A number of athletes have sought "hypnotic" help with varying results. Maury Wills, of the Los Angeles Dodgers, had a leg problem during the 1962 season. "They ached," he said. "Or at least I got it into my head that they ached. I began to worry."

He reported that under "hypnosis" he was told to do exercises and that they would not be painful unless there was something physically wrong with his legs. "It was amazing," he said. "I felt no pain. Of course, some people will say the pain was all in my head in the first place, which is true."

Other athletes have reported absolutely no results from "hypnotic" sessions and that will be the continuing story—failures and successes, depending on the subject and on the "hypnotist."

I worked with a golf pro in the New York area who could no longer make a two-foot putt. I don't play golf and know nothing about the game, but I quickly discovered that the man had simply lost confidence in himself. We talked and I "suggested" ways that he might regain that self-confidence. Soon he was making short putts successfully. "Hypnosis" wasn't the answer, nor was it needed.

A Boston Red Sox pitcher had lost his capability to pitch up to his known ability and came to me, hoping I could help in some way. He asked to be "hypnotized." Instead, we talked about his state of mind when he was pitching well and I discovered that personal problems were at the root of his slipping average. "Hypnosis" could neither have solved these problems nor brought them into sharper focus, aiding him to throw strikes.

Where the claims are totally false for "hypnosis," in my opinion, are in the areas of changing basic personality. It cannot happen with any known techniques. Any change in personality is apt to be temporary no matter what the "hypnotist" suggests. For all of these reasons, at the end of the cycle of interest, medical science practically drops it until the next cycle. Hopefully, something is learned during the peaks of interest.

Predictably, there was considerable hedging in the AMA acceptance. The previously mentioned Dr. Harold Rosen headed the association's committee on "hypnosis" and quickly went on TV channels to discuss the rather abrupt change in AMA's attitude. As an interested observer, I caught him on Art Linkletter's *House Party* and other shows, and read his statements in the press and magazines. He stressed the tremendous dangers of "hypnosis."

No dentist, no psychologist, not even a physician should practice it unless he was also trained in psychiatry, said Dr. Rosen. Above all, it should not be demonstrated on the stage or over TV. The bibles were all but chained. In fact, it almost appeared that no one should practice it except Dr. Rosen. It was a rather astonishing position to take in view of the admitted fact that medical science does not know how "hypnosis" works.

Dr. Rosen maintained that use of "hypnosis" should require a prior in-depth analysis in order to fully understand the subject, or patient. Without such analysis, presumably at going rates, Dr. Rosen claimed that a "hypnotic state" could be "hazardous." Further, he cited cases where, in his judgment, it has caused temporary or permanent damage. One extreme case involved a suicide, resulting from improper "hypnotic" treatment, according to Dr. Rosen.

As a psychiatrist, Dr. Rosen had to know that the only possible scientific way in which to make a definite determination was through an "in-depth" verbal examination of the deceased. But I assume Dr. Rosen did not go to a medium to accomplish this. Therefore, what he distributed to the TV audience had to be more theory than fact, but it sounded factual.

Medicine, unfortunately, joins stage entertainment in vested "hypnotic" interests. As one of its values Dr. Aaron Moss, in his book *Hypnodonture*, states that an "additional fee can be charged." In charging one hundred dollars for a single forty-five minute session to break the smoking habit, Dr. Spiegel cited the reason of not wanting to be "overrun" with patients. A hundred dollars is reasonable enough but the point is—medical "hypnosis" can and does make money.

Writing on the subject, doctors usually make a first-chapter statement that there is "no great mystery about hypnosis," then proceed to drape it in mystery. That's rather human but it does substantiate the ego value in "hypnosis" which seems to go hand in hand with the money value.

With or without the help of Dr. Rosen and the AMA, no person should go to a nonmedical "hypnotist" for a medical problem. If I have an ache, the last person I'll see is my local "hypnotist," and then only to trade reading matter. Medically, in most cases, "hypnosis" has absolutely no value. Of course, I have somewhat the same feeling about many psychoanalysts and psychologists. I have about as much faith in the psychoanalyst's couch as I do in flying carpets, and I'm now appalled at some of the psychology I stuffed into my head, and fully believed, in earlier years.

Since creation, pain has plagued man and the single most fascinating aspect of medical "hypnosis" has been its use as a pain reliever. It has been repeatedly claimed that surgery can be accomplished under "deep trance" without the patient feeling anything, and that dentistry can be accomplished without any sensation of pain. It simply isn't true.

Under so-called "deep hypnosis," the patient is aware of every cut or prick but apparently through his own defensive mechanism rejects it as pain or transfers it or divides it up.

Everything is felt and the polygraph can prove this. Additionally, I've interviewed many patients and not one has denied the "awareness" of pain.

Working as a consultant with a qualified physician, Dr. Robert Stein, I've conditioned more than two dozen expectant mothers to have their children without anesthesia or with very little chemical anesthesia. In postnatal interviews, all admitted being aware of the pain. They either rejected it or transferred it. For instance, we trained one young lady, having her first child, to sing through the labor pains and think of other things. The discomfort diminished, but through her own mechanisms and not mine. She "suggested" her pain away but was not in a "trance," nor under "hypnosis."

In conducting tests with Dr. Barber outside the laboratory, away from more or less controlled responses, we discovered that those people who were able to reject pain accomplished it, basically, in one of three ways: (1) Concentrated on something else—an incident in their lives, a person, a tranquil setting. (2) Made believe they were apart from their bodies. (3) Disbursed the pain.

"I've got to work with it. The pain is here but I'll divide it up over my jaw. It isn't all in one place now." This is not "hypnosis." It is self-generated use of natural *autosuggestion.*

For centuries, mothers and fathers have been practicing a form of it. When a child bumps his head or hurts his hand, the mother often consoles him: "Johnny, you hurt your hand. Let me kiss it. We'll make the boo-boo go away." Depending on the injury and the intensity of the pain, the child is eased; the pain is "sent." But the mother did not produce a "trance" to accomplish it; no words except those of instinct and love. The healing was within.

In early surgery, without anesthesia, an estimated five to ten percent of the patients, according to medical reports, submitted to the knife without moaning or stirring. They seemed to resign themselves and showed little or no outward sign of pain. How did they do it? With no other explanation available, it had to come from within. They apparently handled their situation by natural autosuggestion. This means that the ninety to ninety-five percent who manifested great pain were apparently not capable of utilizing self-suggestion or other mental defensive mechanisms.

Where the emotional leaves off and the physical begins is another admitted unknown, according to medical science. For a time, psychosomatic medicine was simplified to the point that for the laymen it meant that a physical problem created a mental problem or vice versa. Those expert in the field knew differently, soon realizing there was no easy way to isolate the two. We are "whole," totally interconnected. A common cold affects the outlook on life, our mental attitude, as well as the ability to function physically. A toothache is disturbing to the mind function as well as to the physical function.

The human mind may well be the most important key toward working with that "whole."

[12]

Able to pull a rabbit from a hat at the age of ten, practicing levitation before I needed to shave, and having discarded the only crystal ball I ever owned when I was seventeen, I find it hard to buy much of the occult at the age of thirty-seven. But I'm sure I'd feel more kindly toward mediums, seers, stargazers, witches, vampires and werewolves if a sizable portion of the millions of Americans who purchase occult services and wares of one type or another weren't being bilked.

Not everyone who believes in ESP believes in the occult, but every occultist I've ever known, and that numbers quite a few, accepts ESP for fact, often using it to authenticate their own special mystic art. In size, the occult swamps both the interest and endeavor in legitimate psychic phenomena. Out of my library of more than three-thousand titles on psychic phenomena, some two thousand deal exclusively with the occult. They are interesting to read, often amusing, but most, I think, should be placed on the shelf with ghost stories.

With a history dating back almost to the beginning of man, occultism has been a many-tentacled octopus eating away at, and confusing, serious research in telepathy, clairvoyance, psychokinesis and other related fields of ESP. For good reason the general public, as well as a portion of the scientific community not involved in parapsychology exploration, has seldom separated the two distinct areas. Certain to last until man's end, growing as population increases, even spurred by technology backlash, the occult will continue to put gruesome warts on parapsychology, twining in and out of genuine phenomena. With one set of long jeweled fingers on reality, the other hand of the secret arts grasps a combination of religion, folklore, imagination, ignorance, insanity and the unexplainable desire of man to believe in the impossible.

Occult bookshops flourish in all the major cities. The publishing end of occultism alone is worth millions, even to thriving Book-of-the-Month–type clubs. A late check of the paperback racks reveals dozens of titles, from former carnival lion handler Anton Szandor LaVey's *The Satanic Bible* to *Do-It-Yourself Witchcraft*, *The Power of Prayer on Plants* and *The Cosmic Forces of Mu*.

Other available wares would astound an old sorcerer. Ritual potions, oils for concentration and good karma and psychic sex, even aerosol sprays for better prayer are offered, along with black-magic kits and séance kits and apparition kits and such ordinary items as crystal balls, new or used; plans for astral projection; teleporting instructions; formulas for invisibility; and courses in everything from palmistry to the understanding of Zoroastrianism, the ancient Persian religion of fire worship.

What might be considered predictable, youth being explorative as well as easily led, is that the most of the occult buyers, except those who follow astrology and purchase prophetic staples, are under the age of thirty. They are also white, and middle-class, although the occult has its fair share of celebrants in the wealthy suburbs. Many have been to college, and a few pass as intellectuals but appear to be ignoring reality, for the time being. Perhaps that's the name of the whole game.

Hardly surprising is that hippie communes throughout America are reporting many incidents of psychic phenomena. Already pointed in the direction of the paranormal, embracing astrology, reading tarot cards and *I Ching,* the Chinese book of forecast, they are often self-conditioned for imagined experiences in clairvoyance or telepathy. Dr. Krippner, of the Maimonides Dream Laboratory, studied the experiences in twenty-two communes. His findings suggest that mind-altering drugs and yoga-type meditation were no doubt responsible for most of the psychic experiences. When consciousness is altered over an extended period of time, people tend to provide their own frame of reference to validate religious or paranormal occurences.

In mid-June 1972, *Time* magazine devoted a portion of an issue to the occult explosion, terming it a "substitute faith." This is the area that can eventually send bats screaming out of the occult belfry. The other areas seem to rise and fall as crystal balls become cloudy or crack. In addition to LaVey's colorful Church of Satan, duly recognized as a religion and incorporated under California laws, with a membership that cuts a wide but infinitesimal swath in society, there are an estimated hundred, or more, other occult denominations in the United States, all fulfilling metaphysical needs of one sort or another. They vary from old-fashioned spiritualism to nuclear-age science groups. Whatever the brand, they have in common a moneymaking capacity. The occult "clergyman" is often well rewarded.

One of the current fads in the occult field is astral projection. There are psychics and mystics all over the world who flatly claim they can send their "other body," or soul, on exploration or observation trips around the universe, supposedly whistling through space. A few are sincere; some may have produced a manifestation that satisfies *them* as being an actual experience. Hard to swallow, though, is the "other body," in detached form, soaring like an invisible bird. It is either psychosis or a rousing good dream.

However, dreams are a natural, normal form of astral projection. In that sense, all of us take astral trips almost nightly. We are released to mind travel. Fortunately, most of us accept the fact that the mind stays where it should stay, after cavorting a bit, projecting imaginatively; the only body we have remains in bed. We awaken whole, with a good or bad memory of the trip.

Dreams often occur in the early stages of natural sleep, very often when a person is still partially awake, but asleep, too, as we know sleep, which is another scientific mountain to climb. It happens to every normal person—an awareness that you are in a room but still somehow in a dream, too. It can only be attributed, at this point, to mind distortion.

Additionally, most people have occasionally experienced a feeling of "floating away" from themselves when falling asleep. A further infrequent step in the dream state is the actual observation of the detached dreamer—astral projection but nonoccult. A person sees himself from the third-person point of view in all sorts of surroundings, with other persons, known and unknown. Obviously there is sometimes a feedback from the body which increases a type of dream autosuggestion. Also, a type of mental telepathy is sometimes thought to be involved.

Many people have dreamed of levitation; they have seen themselves floating above the ground or running above it, much to their amusement and enjoyment, and much to the amazement of those observing below. One possible explanation is that sleep has made a part of the body dormant; numbness has set in. Even in the half-awake state, the person can feel flotation; he is no longer touching the bed.

This same phenomenon goes a long way toward explaining the yogi who steadfastly believes he has levitated himself after sitting in his yoga position for hours, legs crossed beneath him. Circulation has been cut off. So far as he is concerned, eyes straight ahead or closed in meditation, he has no feeling of roosting on earth. In his mind, where it counts, he is literally floating.

Of all the occult pastimes, astrology is closest to fun. Yet I don't believe we are predestined, which is why I can't resolve star guidance. I treat astrology like perfume: I can savor it but I don't wear it very well.

While I honestly attempt to be charitable about another person's occult beliefs and am often asked, in the question-and-answer period after a college performance, to put blessings on a kinky branch, the only safe reply is, "I don't believe it." Some occultists almost plead for public substantiation, no matter how slim. I can try to fence the question by truthfully saying I'm not an authority or claim I'm not acquainted with that particular cult, or "spirit contact is a phenomena that we, ah . . . don't understand . . ." but the psychic door is left open a crack and a coven of witches fly through.

Once I had a wild idea to gather all the promoters of the occult—the mediums, soothsayers, seers, Satanists, palmists, phrenologists, mind travelers, devils, vampires and voodoo doctors—to a psycho-fest in Madison Square Garden and let them do their things in booths, orchestrated and stage-lit. It might be the greatest show on earth and a bit beyond, entirely commercial. The only drawback I could see was that another two million people would become converts.

[13]

The core of a séance, for good or evil, knowingly fradulent or genuinely believed, is suggestibility. After the conditioning of hymns and holding hands, the sitters are emotionally receptive to signs of the departed ones. If they were not, how could one "sitter" recognize a glowing blue form as her deceased husband? The glowing blue form could be fashioned into any of a thousand different objects, but suggestion directs it to be the late Mr. So-and-so, at least to the eyes of the widow.

If delusion is desired, practically anything is possible in a séance. In a darkened room, after the proper verbal conditioning, usually with religious overtones, the skilled medium can mechanically produce manifestations that are rather convincing. Emotionally charged, the person desiring contact with a deceased loved one is an easy victim.

But manifestations can be produced in a totally dark room without a medium and mechanics. My own experiments, conducted with friends, have produced colors, shapes and movements within twenty minutes. We knew why we were in the room but I was not acting as a medium; I did not speak after the lights went off. The effect was like one of those picture spreads in the *National Geographic* of fish in Stygian black five miles down in the ocean. The manifestations were imagined. They were self-generated by those within the room.

After observing many séances, and having taken part in a few, hoping to learn something, I've never seen or heard anything that would legitimately indicate that one or more persons have ever communicated with the "spirit" of the dead. In some cases, I'm certain the medium steadfastly believed that he or she has penetrated the world beyond. Autosuggestion may play a part in this, the medium acting out a fully believable psychodrama in his or her mind. Or it is possible that telepathy, in which the medium is receiving from the mind of the living "dear one," seated nearby, is involved. Mediums of this type are seldom paid. Their reward is a sick fulfillment. The séance permits the role of God for an hour. But the majority of the "spirit" contacts are staged, cruel put-ons, another of the dangerous games of the occult.

Hypothetically, let's say that the medium does have a capacity to communicate with a deceased person or his "soul." She makes the contact in a darkened room, which is neat theatrics (why not daylight; the "spirit" wouldn't care) and then begins passing information on to the living. In that setting, the information sounds authentic; mainly upbeat, or benign, because the deceased is past all harm or danger. Further, the deceased has achieved an unworldly wisdom, so can give fatherly advice. The séance may broaden as the result of feedback from the living person, human putty at this point, especially if bereaved.

Medium: I see an elderly woman standing by him. She's smiling, as if they belong together.
Widow: Yes, oh, yes! That's his mother. That's Al's mother.
Medium (confidently and soothingly): Yes.

Incredible.

Safely for the medium, it could be Al's deceased mother, sister, favorite aunt, teacher. Most people usually have a "deceased elderly person" somewhere in the background. The medium is not taking much of a chance when seeing "an elderly woman standing by him."

In the earliest known séances, taking place more than two hundred years ago (done for enjoyment and not for "spirit contact"), table legs "rapped," demonstrating the same phenomenon as today's table tilting. They "talked," hence the modern term "table talk." In time the medium took over, and instead of asking "Will it rain tomorrow?" posed "Sam Fuller, do you hear me?" Two raps: Yes.

And although lovable William Fuld, of Baltimore, supposedly "invented" and did indeed patent the ouija board in 1892, almost the same device, called the planchette, was available in France in the seventeenth century. In those days it was thought that a spirit was taking over the body of the player causing the movement of the small wooden piece on the board, providing "yes" or "no" answers, foretelling the future.

The same theory bobbed up in America at the turn of the century, adding weight to the spiritualist movement. Editorials in major newspapers gloomily projected that the ouija board might destroy society and religion, and doom us all. The fad, hot between 1912 and 1916, almost disappeared until it was revived again in a minor way in the thirties and forties. It mushroomed once more in the late sixties when the Parker Brothers bought the Fuld family rights.

One reason for the recurrent and continuing popularity is its game factor and social ramifications—board resting on four knees, with two sets of hands, preferably male and female, involved. Another reason is that it is kin to table tilting, involving *automatism,* genuine physical responses directed by the unconscious. The how and why of automatism is another phenomenon yet to be explained, but it has nothing to do with spiritualism.

Although man has been invoking gods or contacting spirits in one way or another since the beginning of recorded history, the present brand of spiritualism started in America in 1848 and soon became an export. England, never a land to reject ghosts, welcomed the phenomenon.

Two children, the Fox sisters, Catherine and Margaret, of Hydesville, New York, gave birth to the movement with the help of a friendly poltergeist, supposedly the ghost of a man murdered in their sedate old home. His name was "Mr. Splitfoot." He freely communicated with the children on command by rapping on walls and ceilings. The Fox family did not discourage their personable poltergeist but opened the home to demonstrations attended by the press and medical doctors, and eventually the general public. Moreover, he was not a nasty ghost and didn't fling furniture.

The demonstrations were so convincing that a portion of the public both in America and England—those eager to believe not only in a life hereafter but in communication with the dead, a very natural longing—at last had undeniable proof. Spirits existed, could be verbally contacted, and the Fox sisters became the first of many "go-betweens," or mediums.

They didn't get around to confessing it was all a hoax until nearly a half-century later. Catherine admitted the "rappings" came from crackings of their own knee joints. To have this energy reverberate to walls and ceilings sounds implausible unless it is coupled with the subtle conditioning of the witnesses. Simply, they wanted to believe, and then *suggestion* snared them. In most people, surface skepticism was a cover for a deep and ancient desire to accept spirits and spiritualism. The desire is still there.

Sherlock Holmes's creator, Sir Arthur Conan Doyle, took up spiritualism in 1916 at the age of sixty. He claimed to have received a message on attending his first séance but never revealed the message. Later, using his skill as a writer, he endorsed many mediums. Unfortunately, many were revealed to be frauds. And Conan Doyle didn't stop at spiritualism. He maintained that Houdini's feats were not altogether physical; that Houdini dematerialized and then materialized in accomplishing certain routines. Houdini frothed at the idea, though the gentlemen had once been friends.

Chroniclers of Thomas Alva Edison have been remarkably silent about the inventor's interest in psychic phenomena, perhaps judging that facet as damaging to his overall genius. Yet Edison told his friend B. C. Forbes, founder of *Forbes* magazine, that he was intrigued with communication to a life hereafter. On October 20, 1920, *Scientific American* quoted Edison: ". . . if our personality survives, it is strictly logical and scientific to assume it retains memory, intellect, faculties and knowledge that we acquire on this earth. It is reasonable to conclude that those who leave this earth would like to communicate with those left behind . . ."

Edison was apparently serious about inventing an instrument "so delicate as to be affected or moved or manipulated by a personality as it survives in the next life." Such an instrument, when made available, "ought to record something." The inventor never got around to making his "instrument," for which we should perhaps be thankful.

But belief in spiritualism has been universal, from White

House occupants to 10 Downing Street. Abraham Lincoln had some passing interest in spiritualism and did, of record, attend several séances, perhaps only to find out why they were attracting the attention of Mary Todd Lincoln. Canada's Prime Minister William Mackenzie King attended séances to discuss various matters, thought to be personal rather than affairs of state, with his deceased mother. He also claimed to have spoken with his sister Isabel and brother MacDougal.

While I do have a deep personal belief in a hereafter, I remain a steadfast spiritualistic heretic.

[14]

The most famous American spiritualist was the late Reverend Arthur Ford, who achieved overnight fame in January 1929 by supposedly contacting Houdini, who had died three years earlier. Ford had excellent reasons to attempt a séance with the escape artist.

Houdini had spent much time during his last years exposing spiritualists as fakes. Earlier, his beloved mother had passed away while he was in Europe. Houdini often spent seven or eight hours a day prostrate on her grave, carrying on a one-way conversation. Almost insanely bereaved, he went to several mediums to arrange contact. Quickly recognizing hoax, he became enraged. Finally obsessed, he would travel miles to completely shatter the performance of a medium, duplicating every manifestation in broad daylight. His crusade reached the point where he was well on his way to destroy any respectability given to spiritualism.

Not surprisingly, on his death the spiritualists couldn't rest until they proved him wrong, *in absentia,* by making contact with him, and by wresting from him a phantomly apology, plus a sweeping endorsement of their craft from that other disembodied world. One can imagine Houdini having brooded over this long before he died. Contrary to the Tony Curtis movie version of Houdini's life, he did not die in the Chinese Water Torture Cabinet. A student at McGill University in Montreal punched him several times in the stomach, testing Houdini's claims that he could withstand blows if his muscles were set. The punches came as a surprise, and Houdini was not "set." Peritonitis developed and he died on October 31, 1926. Halloween night, of course.

As scientifically as he had planned his jumps between aircraft while handcuffed and his fantastic escapes, he had planned his "escape" from the mediums in death. He gave his wife, Beatrice, a code, with the understanding that unless these specific words—*pray, answer, say, now, tell, please, speak, quickly, look, be quick*—were used, it would be but one more example of the spiritualistic mantrap.

Until the Reverend Ford's séance, no medium had broken the code despite their unearthly powers. It is safe to guess that hundreds attempted legitimately and a number would no doubt have traded a shipload of rapping tables to have come up with the information by any means. A few reportedly tried by breaking and entering.

The Reverend Ford, according to his own account, had discovered his psychic powers in 1924 during a meditation session in New York with Swami Yogananda. He went into a trance and suddenly began talking with a French accent. The "voice" belonged to "Fletcher," a French-Canadian Catholic who had been killed in World War I. Ford had played with "Fletcher" as a child, and the voice from beyond became Ford's constant spiritual *control,* or *guide.* Sir Conan Doyle took credit for having persuaded Ford to become a professional medium in 1927.

Then came the startling news that Bess Houdini had called Walter Winchell, the New York columnist, to say that the great Arthur Ford had communicated with Harry Houdini, and that he had repeated the ten words to her. If anything on earth would prove that spirit communication was possible, this was

174

definitely it. Mediums the world over were jubilant and Arthur Ford was superheroic. Not for long. Within a matter of weeks, Bess retracted the statement and said there was no evidence of any communication with her husband.

As the puzzling story developed, it became known that the widow had been ill during the period of Ford's séance. Lucidity became a question. Further, one of the nurses attending Mrs. Houdini was a friend of Arthur Ford's. This also tended to cloud the breaking of the code. However, persons close to Bess later declared that the nurse was not involved.

Few people seemed to take into account the fact that the code had already appeared in print the previous year. With the help of author Harold Kellock, Bess Houdini had written a warm, indulgent biography of her husband, revealing the ten words. In effect, Bess had already made it impossible for the spiritualists to prove anything. Ford had only to read the book entitled *Houdini* to make good his claim of spirit contact with the former Ehrich Weiss.

Ford's attempt was not the first or the last. By nature, magicians are curious people. Though they may not buy spiritualism, they cannot resist probing it. Following the deaths of the Great Carter and Thurston in 1936, Harry Blackstone not only tried to communicate with them but also tried to contact Houdini again. On May 12, 1936, Blackstone said, "We were agreed to wait until we felt conditions were right. Tonight is the night. Success or failure? That, of course, I cannot tell." He failed, but his statement indicates that he did discuss the future attempt with both Carter and Thurston in some detail.

It is also known that Carter had previously waited for some message from Houdini, although he maintained, along with the escape artist, that spirit contact was a myth. During two stage performances, Carter reported that he did "hear" four taps in an effects cabinet which could not be explained. He tapped back but received nothing more and later was inclined to believe that it was a freak incident, or that he had imagined it, rather than his friend's communication in Morse code.

Over the years, Arthur Ford continued to insist that he had contacted Houdini. It tended to lend credence to spiritualism and bothered me for personal reasons beyond a disbelief in mediums. As the fictitious incident was renewed again and again within spiritualistic circles, there was never any recognition of Houdini's passionate hatred of the go-betweens. Finally, in 1966 I contacted Ford, inviting him to duplicate his earlier "success" in full public view on television. I reasoned that it could be duplicated because Houdini hadn't gone any "farther out" since 1929, or my understanding of spiritualism was that time did not decrease the possibility of contact.

I did not hear from Ford but was dumfounded when Ford performed a séance on television with Bishop James A. Pike, supposedly contacting Pike's deceased son, on September 17, 1967. I flew to Canada to examine the film which appeared on a show titled *Perry's Probe*. I ran it back and forth for hours, then attempted to unravel the prior relationship between Pike and Ford, if any. Their TV appearance had been arranged by Allen Spraggett, religious editor of the Toronto *Star*.

It was not the first time the controversial bishop had been involved in a séance. Pike had been party to several séances conducted by members of Ford's organization, without Ford present. Whether Pike was taking part in the séances at that time because of a belief in spiritualism or simply investigating it is not known. Ford and Pike finally met outside a church in New York.

On *Perry's Probe*, it all begins quite innocently and it is very possible that Bishop Pike had no knowledge that Ford planned a séance. The two men are discussing things in general, conversing in the manner of any talk or panel show; then suddenly Ford goes into a trance and announces he is in communication with Pike's son, who had committed suicide the previous year.

"Fletcher," the constant other-world companion, was again the guide to Pike's son. In viewing the film, it is almost as if "Fletcher" is Ford, the usual routine, fitting himself to the responses of Bishop Pike. There is a noticeable feedback of information. The more you listen to, and look at, the film, the more aware you become of the feedback. It went something like this:

Ford: I see him, he is with someone in England.
Pike: Oh, yes, yes, that's a teacher of his.

Later, in Pike's book about the Ford séances, we are told that Ford communicated the presence of the teacher. The fact is, *Pike told Ford about the teacher.* In my opinion it was controlled, or developed, information, not free information grabbed from the "other side."

In studying the film of *Perry's Probe*, it is interesting to see just how much information Biship Pike was giving away by his rate of breathing, signs of excitability and lurchings of his body. The experienced medium can read these signs as a doctor reads a heartbeat. He targets on any scrap of information he can develop.

Fortunately it was Pike himself who finally said, of that particular night, "Maybe it wasn't spiritualism; maybe it was telepathy." I hope he meant telepathy from-Pike-to-Ford. An occultist for more than fifty years, Ford would have been remiss not to develop telepathic communication.

Ford said that a second séance was held several months later in Philadelphia and that more information from Pike's son was developed, enabling Pike to write *The Other Side*, but supposedly many things were left out of the book because they were too personal and intimate to print. *Pike became a convert and enthusiastically embraced certain areas of the mystic sciences.* Pike, the thinker, the scholar. Baffling.

But after the Pike séance in Canada, I could not resist again inviting Reverend Ford to demonstrate his psychic powers on

TV. He had now voluntarily indicated a willingness to perform in front of cameras. So I persuaded Mike Douglas to grant ninety minutes for a taping. Ford would be able to set his own conditions, except that it would have to be on film for later analysis. He had previously said that he would not work on "live TV" because his gift couldn't be "turned on" that way, so Mike agreed to lose the studio audience. Besides, Ford would be paid.

In order to convince the public that no "confederates" would be used, no *controlled* information available, I suggested that we bring in a reporter from the Philadelphia *Inquirer* with names of deceased persons from the news-clip morgue. They would not be famous persons. Consequently, the medium could not be accused of using sources of readily available information. The Reverend Ford could have his pick, trying one after the other until he achieved success. The news-clip file could then be used, on the spot, to identify friends, associates and relatives of the deceased. I was to stay on the sidelines as an observer.

A friend of Ford's, whom I later met, was in the medium's home in Miami when the wire arrived. He said Ford winced and went on about his other business. After the sensational Pike episode in Toronto, I'm sure he did not care to air séances. This time, though, he formally declined on the grounds that he would not appear with an entertainer. I was amused more than having my feelings hurt.

Ford again got into the act when Bishop Pike was reported missing in the Israeli desert. Ford stated that he went into deep meditation and saw Pike in a cave. A few days later Diane Pike, the bishop's wife, reported a vision in which she saw her husband leave his body and ascend to a large crowd of people.

Incidents such as the various Bishop Pike "contacts" are extremely difficult to bury. They lend themselves to repeats. The British psychic and medium Ena Twigg, with whom I spent an interesting afternoon in Chicago, let it be known that she had contacted the bishop himself after his emergence on the "other side." Previously, she had claimed contacts with Pike's son, joining Ford and an American medium named George Daisley as the selected go-betweens with the younger Pike.

According to Mrs. Twigg, her tape-recorded contact with Bishop Pike occurred prior to the time his body was found on the Israeli desert. In the recording, Dr. Pike's voice is supposedly relayed through Mrs. Twigg, who was in a trance state. Several witnesses reportedly attended the séance and posed questions, which the bishop reportedly answered.

Acknowledging the "evidence" of *Perry's Probe* film and the tapes of Mrs. Twigg, I remain skeptical. And it is safe to wager that the bishop will be contacted again and again by one medium or another. His prominence and his pre-death involvement in spiritualism guarantee he'll be a target for many years to come, joining that erstwhile nonbeliever, Harry Houdini.

I do not go about tossing challenges, having done it but twice in twenty-odd years, but in both the Dr. Spiegel "hypnotic test" and the Ford case I couldn't resist in the name of reason.

[15]

Because of the potential damage to many people, prophecies, especially the doomsday variety that appear in news columns, have always made me uneasy. Despite the celebrated Jeane Dixon and others, prophecy is basically an occult area. Linked with astrology, it is probably the oldest secret art.

Although I've abandoned even the amateur practice of it, I've made predictions from cold calculation and pure guess to prove that is is possible to be a "seer" by following and analyzing news events, playing percentages and making use of actuarial tables. Successful prophecy also requires making more than one prediction for a designated period of time. Odds are that one or two out of three or four prophecies will be "hits."

Back in 1965, while appearing at the Weldwood Lounge, a night club on the Scranton-Carbondale Highway in Pennsylvania, I predicted stories that would appear in the Friday, April 9, issue of the Scranton *Tribune*. The predictions were made on April 2 and handed to WDAU-TV commentator Nancy Dolphin. It was done for publicity purposes.

First prediction: Headline, page 1, "collision kills driver, demolishes car. A 22-year-old man or woman will be involved."

Second prediction: "Robber in gun battle with police."

Third prediction: "Eighteen-year-old Negro terrorized."

I added a general statement: "The car crash tragedy may be pushed off the front page by the Health-Welfare Bill vote. If so, the House of representatives will pass it by approximately 200 votes."

The outcome was as follows in the *Tribune* of April 9:

1. Headline, page 1: "City Man Dies in Car Crash." The overline said: "Small Foreign Car Demolished." In the first paragraph, it was revealed that the driver was twenty-two years old.

2. Headline, page 1: "Robber in Store Holds Off Police Three Hours."

3. Top headline, page 2: "Arrest 2 Cops for Terrorizing Negro."

An Associated Press story, date-lined Washington, also on page 1, stated that the House passed the Health-Welfare measure by 198 votes.

Analyzing the "hits," it is rather safe to predict that in an area the size of Scranton, a fatal car crash will occur within almost any overnight period. The guess at the victim's age was luck. If I had not been right about the age, the reader would dismiss it, being satisfied by the fact that I'd hit the accident itself.

The second prediction was equally guided by calculation but had a larger potential to miss. I carefully did not say that the "robber would be in a store or hold off the police for three hours." A safety factor was that I did not specifically name Scranton. The incident could have taken place in Philadelphia to validate the prediction.

The third prediction also stemmed from calculation. There had been racial unrest in the Scranton area for some weeks. As I recall, the victim of alleged police brutality was not eighteen years old but this prophecy miss was overlooked. The main prediction had come true.

My footnote to the predictions on the House vote was ferreted from several news stories out of Washington that appeared around April 2. They forecast that the bill would pass by approximately 200 votes.

In discussing the accuracy of the predictions with reporters, I said that I made "no claim to psychic ability and that the prophecies were based on logic." But statements of this sort, I've learned, are lost in the more sensational disclosures of the seer.

On Tuesday, August 15, 1967, a story by Louis Effrat appeared on the sports pages of the *New York Times* crediting me with predicting the post positions of the following Saturday night's $100,000 International Trot at Roosevelt Raceway. I'd selected Roquepine, Grainella and Real Speed for one, two and three post positions as a dual publicity venture for the raceway and myself. However, I did not gaze into a crystal ball to come up with the order of the trotting horses. Cold calculation largely provided the answers.

As a further example of this nonprofessional "seer talent," I took on the task of prophecy for TV's *Joey Bishop Show*, promising to predict stories that would appear in the Los Angeles *Times* on the day of the Bishop program.

Studying two weeks of the *Times*, front to back, I attempted to forecast events simply by trends in the news, then I made three predictions a week ahead, as with the Scranton perform-

THE AMAZING WORLD OF KRESKIN

ance. They were sealed in an envelope and given to Inspector Sherwood Black of the Los Angeles County Sheriff's Department.

The day of the show, Bishop, a bit antsy, called to ask if I'd hit them. By then, I'd seen the morning paper but refused to reveal the predictions. Bishop kept saying, "Milton Berle wants to know, too." I was pleased that Milton Berle was interested but felt that Bishop should react spontaneously on camera. He was exasperated but had to go along with it. I seldom discuss what I'm going to do with anyone, unless technical help is needed, and I seldom reveal any results until they are shown onstage. It goes back, I'm sure, to the magic training.

The time arrived, and the detective opened the envelope. Bishop whooped when the *Times* headline matched the prediction almost word for word. I'd also called the editorial-page subject correctly, but the third prediction—that a story on the transport of Army nerve gas would appear inside the paper— wasn't in either edition I'd checked that morning. However, the inspector spoke up to say that he thought there was a third edition. During the commercial break, someone located it and on page 5 was a story of nerve-gas movement.

Once again I appeared to be a miraculous prophet but it was entirely deduction, along with some luck. A major event could have broken to push the headline and the nerve-gas account out of the paper. I would have failed. But with similar research, any non-prophet, particularly an experienced newspaperman, could have done the same thing. Indeed, I believe most prophecy is based on deduction and logic rather than vision.

My amateur dabbling, a thing of the past, has never involved personalities or doomsday events, and I become ill when a seer predicts the death of a famous person. In the present climate, forecasting death is placing a gun in the hands of some pathetic paranoid who needs only this justification to begin his stalk. In print, the death has been decreed. Beyond this possibility, even the most secure, hardened political leader or world figure would have to be affected at least momentarily by reading of his imminent death. And newspapers seemingly cannot resist passing the bad news along. However, I realize it is "news" of a sort. But there are indications that both the press and television are awakening to the dangers.

Not long ago a famed seer was scheduled to appear on the *Tonight Show* and his shocking moment of glory was to be a prediction that one of America's best-known political figures was to suffer a tragedy. On learning the politician's name, the Carson staff wisely declined. (No, it was not George Wallace.) Happily, the tragedy hasn't occurred thus far.

It is claimed, perhaps with some validity, that fortunetelling, spread over the receptive millions, is probably harmless: "You'll meet a beautiful girl and live happily ever after." Yet untold thousands have suffered mental anguish because of a seer's reading. In some cases, disaster and tragedy can be directly linked to foretelling without the occult nonsense of predestining the event. My answer is always the same when someone asks, "Can you recommend a reputable seer?" I don't know one.

One morning I was ushered into the dressing room of a famous actress. We were to appear shortly on the same show. She was distraught and had been crying. She said, "I have to ask you something. I'm very much in love with this man. But I've been told not to marry him." I begged off, lightly saying I left that type of advice to "Dear Abby" or Joyce Brothers. Then I found she'd gone to a celebrated Hollywood soothsayer the previous night. He did readings with cards and had "seen" her future: *If you marry this man, the first four years of your life will be divinely happy but something terrible will happen in the fifth year. You both will be devastated.*

No matter how divinely happy she would have been the first four years, the fifth "cursed" year, if the prediction was believed, would have been approached with misgiving and suspicion. Any quarrel might be blown out of proportion by

memory of the prediction. Worse, the actress definitely believed in the occult or she wouldn't have gone to the soothsayer
in the first place.

Although I made an effort to point out that I thought all
such predictions were ridiculous, she decided not to marry the
man. Eventually she went to another well-known fortuneteller.
This time the advice was even gloomier. After a while she lost
her TV series and her present life is a mess. Month by month,
and even allowing for deep neurosis on her part, it can be
traced back to the first soothsayer.

There appear to be two kinds of future; the *controlled future*
and the *free future*. They are probed by the fortunetellers of
one specialty or another—astrologists, numerologists, phrenologists, palmists and other categories. Reading devices range
from crystal balls and tarot cards to wrinkled handkerchiefs.
Tea leaves, of course. I know one man who reads beer suds.

Predictions of the controlled future, such as events, appear
to be largely calculated. Past incidents forecast future incidents. Although the public often seems to be impressed, it is
hardly a display of mystic power to forecast an earthquake
along the San Andreas Fault when seismologists already have
made the prediction based on technical data. Nor is it
particularly impressive to forecast a "war in the Middle East"
or a revolution in Latin America. Within a given time span,
odds are on the side of the prophet.

Predictions of the free future category, not tied directly to
events past or present, plucked out of the ether, are somewhat
a grand gamble. They are also notable for failure. California
did not slide into the Pacific a few years back, one of the
wackiest prophecies of the century, probably spawned by a
geologist's casual remark. Even those that appear to be a
brilliant success eventually seem to fall into question and
doubt.

Jeane Dixon's prediction that Russia would send an object
into space was in the "free future" category, at first glance.
There were no closely related events at the time. Sputnik went

up and so did Mrs. Dixon's reputation. It was a startling, brilliant "hit." But later analysis, certain to come, raised the question of government knowledge of Russian activity in early space research and Mrs. Dixon's wide contacts in Washington. Science was not totally unaware of the Russian preparations.

Mrs. Dixon's innate goodness, sincerity and firm belief in her predictions are not in doubt. She may well have psychic abilities; she may well have developed hers to an exceptional degree. She admits to the use of telepathy. Perhaps some information is gained in this manner. But prior information, gained in any manner, does not produce what the general public labels and accepts as "pure prophecy"—visions untainted by related factual events.

Previously Mrs. Dixon had predicted that China would go Communist, but so did a number of State Department analysts. She predicted the defeat of Thomas Dewey by Harry Truman; the landslide election of Dwight Eisenhower, the fall of Nikita Khrushchev and the suicide of Marilyn Monroe. Her batting average has been good, but some of these events were predictable by trend. Beautiful Miss Monroe was a rather good candidate for tragedy, and Khrushchev's ouster did not astonish knowledgeable diplomats. The Harry Truman victory was a remarkable prediction, however, whether visionary, telepathic or based on a Washington cocktail-party hunch.

Mrs. Dixon, who in private life is a real estate broker, is probably best known for her prophecy that John Kennedy would die in office. In a May 1956 *Parade Magazine* issue, she forecast that whoever was elected President in 1960 would be a Democrat, have blue eyes and die in office. Putting aside the "blue eyes," by the late fifties there was a better than even chance that the next President would be a Democrat. After eight years of a Republican administration, with President Eisenhower retiring, the odds were tipped toward the out-party in this controlled future.

Additionally, many numerologists around the world predicted that the "1960 President" would die in office because of the curious fact that every President, except the first two, who was elected in a "zero" year did not finish his term. By 1976, the numerologists are certain to forecast that the 1980 President is doomed. Name unknown, he has already been eliminated.

However, in analyzing the Dixon forecasts, she also, weeks before the 1960 election, predicted that Richard Nixon would be the winner. In the biography by Ruth Montgomery, Mrs. Dixon is quoted as insisting that Nixon would have won had there been a recount. It presents a dilemma: Does she want credit for predicting the "recount" winner or predicting that the Democrat would die? The Greek oracles tended to work this way, taking advantage of whatever prediction came true. Even Nostradamus, the champion of all, stayed vague too.

Prior to Kennedy's departure for Dallas, Mrs. Dixon said that she saw "war clouds" over the White House. After the fact, this vision could be interpreted to mean something other than armed conflict. It could be read as trouble of any kind, linked to events. Dallas newspapers had reflected a climate that wasn't favorable and this was reflected, in turn, by the Washington press. Several of Kennedy's advisers had cautioned him against the trip. This, too, was known. An ominous future for JFK had some fact as foundation.

The Jeane Dixon successes have been much publicized; her failures have been lost in the onward rush of the news. She predicted that President Johnson would die in office, that Hubert Humphrey would succeed him, and that the Vietnam war would end in the spring of 1968. Of her ten major predictions for 1968, not one came true.

Among her most interesting 1970 predictions: Ambassador Sargent Shriver would win a governorship; George Wallace would again obtain political office but his effort for the presidency will be neutralized by forces emanating from the Senate; Fidel Castro would be physically removed from Cuba sometime that year.

Her "hits" included: No peace in Vietnam (that year); Vice-President Agnew rising in stature; Prime Minister Eisaku

THE POWER OF SUGGESTION

Sato would lead Japan to greater prosperity; continuing problems with Latin America, especially Cuba; defense spending would increase.

Certain people seem to have developed a high sensitivity to perceive information in a manner that is not common. They might be called "psychics." Likewise, some of the manifestations of the "medium" could be explained by clairvoyance or telepathy as opposed to spirit contact. In that sense, I do believe in some "psychics." Particularly, I'm inclined to believe in those who practice and explore the field scientifically, separating religious aspects; the tinkering of the usual "medium."

Although the late Eileen Garrett, founder of the Parapsychology Institute in 1951, was often called a "medium," she was no doubt a true psychic, in the above sense. "I have a gift, a capacity—a delusion, if you will—called 'psychic,' " she said. "I have been called many things from a charlatan to a miracle woman. I am, at least, neither of these."

Her psychic abilities, first discovered in childhood, seemed to lie in clairvoyance, healing (though it could not be described as faith healing in the religious application) and perception of auras or field consciousness. Mrs. Garrett continually stressed her acute sensory abilities.

But notably, the "gift," as she described it, underwent long training. She spent five years at the British College of Psychic Science in London, and put in another five years of grueling work and preparation in all aspects of psychic research. She was not a charlatan.

[16]

On the first rehearsal of a Flip Wilson TV show, the comedian threw up his hands in a warding-off fashion and howled, "Don't touch me!"

I had started toward him.

Everyone laughed.

Flip said, "You think I'm kiddin'? Leave my brain alone."

He got another laugh, which was the purpose, but there are times when I almost feel as if I'm back in Baron's store in Bethlehem, flashing *porabiti,* the "evil eye." I can sympathize with Mrs. Garrett.

Very much aware that I'm often considered a bit different, I realize that people sometimes tend to be uncomfortable around me, as if I had invisible antennas. *Mr. Spock has come to visit from Vulcan.*

Strangers often lump me with psychics and mediums. Some people suspect I'm continually reading minds. There's always the person who will come up to demand, "Tell me what I'm thinking."

I've had drunks say, "Levitate me."

I'm asked to read fortunes, predict stocks; call the winners of football games and horse races. I patiently explain that if I could predetermine the Kentucky Derby or foretell a hot stock I wouldn't be spending as much time on jets or coping with night owls at a 2 A.M. Vegas lounge performance.

Usually I'm successful at laughing my way out of it or changing the subject, but I never really win. I'm the performer who won't perform in private, the expert who dodges. However, I don't know any professional entertainer who doesn't have the same problem.

There are also the "how do you do it?" people. They want to know, step by step, how telepathy works, and if psychokinesis is possible. I don't blame them. But I either have to sound inadequate by admitting that I don't really know or attempt an explanation about what is known, which can never be satisfying and would take half the night.

So I do try to by-pass parties unless I'm a paid performer. Additionally, I have to stand around with a soft drink and appear to be enjoying myself. I'm not against social drinking, but gin and thought perception do not mix. Drugs might provide a synthetic sensitivity, or afford trips of a kind, but I prefer natural methods. Despite numerous recommendations, the praises of the late Aldous Huxley, Timothy Leary and others, I've never tried LSD, nor do I intend to. I have too much respect for the human brain to turn it into a biscuit on a rainbow.

I do get myself into messes sometimes, mainly through a combination of innocence and stupidity. After an opening night in Vegas I had to do a "command" appearance at a management party. Showing off a bit, I took out a deck of cards, selected one, displayed it, and then shoved it back into the deck about thirty-two cards down, then riffled the deck without lifting it from my hand, producing the selected card now in the top position. (It's pure sleight of hand but thus far, even with slow-motion cameras, no one has caught the transfer.) There was applause and I then shuffled the deck, cut it several times, and dealt three hands of poker, one hand of which I knew would contain four aces and a king. Again, it was manipulation but done faster than the eye could follow. I performed it several times, the aces and the king always hitting in the same hand.

About twenty minutes later a sleepy-eyed observer drew me aside. "Say, Mr. Kreskin, I'll give you $15,000 to sit in with me tomorrow night." I refused, of course, but he kept calling every day for almost a week. That brought about a decision to stop performing card effects, except for lounge audiences, anywhere in the state of Nevada.

I seem to have a problem with cards in Nevada. Although I was irked for a while, I'm now only amused that I'm banned from playing blackjack at the Flamingo casino in Vegas. My ban, not the first for someone who works in the mentalist area, resulted from a night when I ran some money to six times its original amount in about an hour. However, I did not use any form of ESP as was implied by the Flamingo. I was playing from memory of the cards, an awareness of the odds and how the deck changed as it was dealt. The secret in any card game, bridge to blackjack, is casing the deck.

In blackjack, when a card is tossed off the deck, the odds of another card of that value coming up again immediately lessen. As each four or five leaves the deck, the statistical odds move to the favor of the player if he remembers the values of the played cards. As an example, if all the fives remain in the deck, I rarely bet anything but the minimal count I allot myself for playing each hand.

As they are played, all cards should be mentally filed away to keep the deck in favor of the player. As the higher cards come into his favor, it is time to play the high bids. When the deck remains in favor of the house, the wise blackjack player will stay with a minimal bet.

Obviously, when the "pit man," the game boss, realizes that the player is casing the deck, memorizing it as it is played, he'll instruct the dealer to shuffle the cards more as the deck reaches the halfway point. When it becomes apparent that even shuffling will not favor the house odds, the pit man usually requests the player to remove himself from the table, which is what happened to me at the Flamingo. In fairness, no casino welcomes anyone in my field. The pit bosses have nervous spasms.

But since I do enjoy blackjack, I'm permitted to play at the Nugget in Reno. I reached an agreement with Jim Thompson, the casino boss, and owner John Escuaga that I'd never play for more than an hour, and never bet more than five dollars a hand. But during one engagement there, using the casing system, I played for twenty-one straight mornings, usually between four and five, after my last show in the lounge. I kept a record of my winnings and found I'd multiplied my original five dollars into four hundred times that amount. The casing system does work.

•   •   •

One area, not involving cards, that I've completely abandoned is pickpocketing. For a long while I used it as a warm-up when appearing before businessmen's groups. Mingling with the audience prior to the banquet and show, I'd lift a wallet and then single that person out later to ask, "Could I borrow a dollar bill, please?" While he was frantically patting his pockets, I'd turn to a subject onstage and make a similar request. As he began to reach, I'd ask, "Sir, do you always carry two wallets? What's that bulge in your side pocket?"

It backfired several times when a subject would discover his wallet was missing prior to the show. Once, at a Philadelphia smoker, a victim of this exercise called the police before I could return his money. He was irate. I've also stopped lifting watches, which was a variation of the pickpocket routine. Both were leftovers from the magic-act days.

Yet it is often difficult to separate the stage from the offstage, and when my act featured "hypnosis" I'd be called on now and then to perform away from the spotlight. When an entertainer is struggling up, it isn't wise to turn down a club owner's request. "Kres, my wife wants to stop smoking. How about helping her?" I remember treating one such lady, suggesting that the cigarettes would taste horrible (which isn't the way to go about it) and even the smell of smoke would be sickening. The lady awakened me the next morning to say that she still had the desire and what could she do about not being able to keep food down. Eventually I quit that medical area.

But there is always the temptation to be helpful. Appearing in Baltimore at the start of the World Series between the Orioles and the Pittsburgh Pirates, I was asked by the mayor to give a mental assist to the home team. I replied, innocently enough, "Tell them to think positively."

The mayor's PR man apparently took the advice to local papers. The next day stories appeared on the sports page that "Kreskin, the mentalist, told the people of Baltimore to think positively," implying that half a million minds could put the

Orioles over the top. I even saw street signs that said: "THINK POSITIVELY FOR THE BIRDS."

They lost, three games to four, and flying to Louisville after the final game, I sat beside a man from Baltimore. We began to talk and he said, "Oh, you're the guy . . ."

And every entertainer has gone through the period when he attempts to impress friends offstage, usually for laughs. In a restaurant I'd ask the waitress to concentrate on an important date in her life and then go back to the kitchen and write it down. I'd jot the date on a calling card and pass it to my dinner companion. On return, the waitress would be flustered when the two dates, usually the birthday, matched. It would be worth a few minutes of laughs and awe. Fortunately I grew out of that ego routine too.

Although I really prefer college audiences to all others, because of their eager response, club dates are often fun, too. Other performers, band leaders, waiters and waitresses, stagehands, become friends. There's that traditional "inside" atmosphere, a crazy climate all its own, which is welcome after a run of campus and town-hall dates. Show-business camaraderie is of course unlike any other and hasn't changed much in a century or more. Now and then something typically "show biz" will occur to afford a moment of warmth and satisfaction.

I was walking down the main street of Reno one morning when I spotted Ralph Young, of the singing team of Sandler & Young, on the opposite side of the street. I yelled over but he didn't answer back. He opened his mouth and pointed to his throat. Knowing that they were scheduled to open that night at the Nugget, I crossed the street. In barely more than a whisper, Ralph said he'd gotten over an allergy attack but had lost his voice. His doctor had told him that there was no apparent physical reason and had suggested that he seek psychological help. Young was thinking of flying to Los Angeles to see a "hypnotist." He was ready to cancel the show, even though the team was due onstage in about ten hours.

I reasoned that if the loss of voice was psychological, Young would have to provide his own cure, with or without help. I requested he call his doctor for approval. We met in his dressing room about an hour later and I told him I thought he might respond to suggestion on an unconscious level and convince himself that he could recover his voice. After proving that he was capable of response, I taught him a simple, progressive exercise which lasted no more than thirty seconds, then left the dressing room. I talked to him once more before show time and had the feeling that he had licked the problem. When the spotlight hit Sandler & Young that night, Ralph was relaxed, smiling, and sang with his usual ease. Without invading psychiatric territory, I'd administered a simple mental cough drop and felt good about it.

There are fun times. Playing the Hilton in Vegas, I kept getting an intriguing but distracting thought. I also had the feeling that four separate sets of eyes were staring at me, literally locked on. They seemed to be well in the shadows at the back of the lounge. I did say, once, "I don't know who you are but I'll talk to you later." There was low female laughter from several points at the back of the room.

After the show was over and the room had cleared, the waitresses came up, smiling widely. One said, "Did you get it, Kres? We decided to send you a single thought. You a good lover?"

They all four broke up in laughter. We kept the gag running for a week and then I was off to Los Angeles.

A personal life is difficult. Romance, if that word is still acceptable in these days of Women's Lib, is a problem and I'm unmarried. For one thing, almost constant travel forces telephone friendships, and here-tonight-gone-tomorrow evenings. Yet there is another difficulty which involves, in a way, ESP. Take a new date out, find her attractive and fun, and at one point in the evening there is a suspicious look and a question that is not altogether kidding. "Kres, are you reading my mind?"

Not guilty. But projecting that slight suspicion into marriage and placing myself in a wife's shoes, I can see that it would be something of a burden. A women's page editor once asked, "Would you apply *suggestibility* in a marital situation?" I replied, "No, I wouldn't do anything like that." I'm certain I would. I'm human, as prone to self-protection as anyone else.

I am guilty of sensing certain things. In ordinary conversation I tend to read eyes and breathing rates. I do it automatically, without thought. The only advantage is the tip-off when someone is becoming tense or bored or wants to change the subject. Most people "read" the same signs automatically. Perhaps my reaction is a little quicker.

I do carry over some habits from the stage, although I attempt to guard against them. Without really being aware of it, I usually walk to the left of anyone, circling around them if I find myself on the right. It's disconcerting, I'm sure, but I work to my right when doing a concert, simply a habit, and always work to my right when being telepathically "guided" toward a hidden object.

I'm also inclined to jot things down on a slip of paper, simply to remember them. Understandably, scribbling makes a dinner guest uneasy and is insulting. So is rolling a coin back and forth across the knuckles of my hand. I've been doing it since childhood and occasionally do it today, quite unconsciously. It's a nervous habit. If I'm talking to someone and suddenly realize that they are studying my hand, I can be certain that a quarter is riding the humps of the knuckles. It usually happens when I'm waiting to go onstage or fidgeting around in an office.

Memory, offstage, is a continuous problem. I think I compensate, purposely, for the deep concentration required by work. I forget names, misplace papers or keys, and what is most embarrassing, have missed dinner or business appointments. I must write them down; then they seem to by-pass the psychological block.

Although it isn't a part of what I do now, I believe I could still do memory routines in front of an audience. I learned how in high school. My brother Joe used to wheel out a blackboard, and I'd call a teacher to the stage to write down twenty-five or thirty words, numbering each one as the audience called them out. I'd take one look, then turn my back to the board, matching the correct numbers with the words the teacher read out loud. However, I now feel pretty ridiculous when I go into a large lot and can't remember where my car is parked. I can read the expression on my date's face while I look helplessly around: *Some mentalist.*

One result of this applied poor memory offstage is that Lou Reda lays out my schedules precisely, and on paper, as to plane departures, hotel accommodations, local contacts, telephone numbers, where and when I'm supposed to appear. Often complicated, sometimes requiring five or six flights a week from coast to coast, the schedules look like battle plans.

But as generals and admirals have discovered, there are times when the best of battle plans go completely awry. Let us call this *Concert Tour No. 1, 1973:*

In good spirits, I arrived at Newark Airport at 7:15 A.M. for a flight to Detroit, scheduled to arrive at 9:30, enabling an 11 A.M. concert in Grosse Point, Michigan. For the first time I was accompanied by a travel manager, Sam Lasagio, simply because of complexities of twelve shows in eight days.

Approaching Gate 17, I was recognized by the airline's smiling key man at Newark. He took me in tow. The chief security man also recognized me, said something about being sure that I wasn't a hijacker and waved us all through, falling in behind. We went to the coffee shop, guests of the genial airline representative, who said we'd eventually board through Gate 21; just relax.

Over coffee and jokes, I glanced at the big clock over the counter now and then until my new travel manager, looking out of the window, said, "Isn't that our plane taking off?" The airline man and the security chief promptly disappeared. The big clock was slow.

I no longer trust genial airline greeters.

After a frantic private helicopter ride to La Guardia, American Airlines worked out a schedule to get us to Detroit by 12:15 P.M. The concert finally began about one o'clock. I had some difficulty establishing rapport with my audience.

The next stop was Hillsdale, Michigan, for a concert at Hillsdale College. We drove there late that same day and were met by the sponsors. One said, "We're sorry you're late for the press conference. They've all gone home."

I asked, "What press conference?"

It was a great start, particularly when I found out that the doors were to open at 6:30 for a show we'd scheduled for 9:15. I'd requested, selfishly, the late time instead of the usual 8 P.M. to be able to watch a Flip Wilson show in which I'd made several appearances. This meant they'd twiddle their thumbs for three hours.

"Didn't you tell the public that it was a nine-fifteen curtain?" I asked. The contract had been written up that way.

"Well, there was a rumor to that effect," he answered. "But don't let it bother you. We've set up TV's in the auditorium so everybody can watch it with you."

I groaned.

Hastings was next. At one o'clock the following afternoon a car drove up to the motel. The Michigan booking agent had sent his eighteen-year-old son, Mike, to take us from Hillsdale to Hastings. The car was loaded with sound equipment. The back seat was crammed. So was the trunk. Huge boxes of amplifiers and speakers, enough to handle The Grateful Dead.

"I'm not a rock-and-roll performer," I said. "All I need is two mikes, a table, a chair and a small folding screen. Why do we have all this?"

"My dad thought we should come prepared," Mike said.

So the three of us mashed into the front seat and set out for Hastings. What was supposed to be two hours turned into four. Worse, the heater couldn't be adjusted. It was a constant ninety degrees in the car. I thought our shoes would melt.

Arriving at the Chamber of Commerce building, I was promptly told, "The press left about a half-hour ago."

"What press?" I asked.

They said, "Oh, TV, a radio station and the local newspaper."

"No one told me." We could have left at noon.

Everyone had a blank look.

While I tried to square myself with the press over the phone, Sam and the booker's son went to the school auditorium to check it out. They returned to say that the sound equipment was handled by the custodians and wouldn't work.

"See," Mike grinned. "My dad was right." He set up the rock-and-roll system.

We had Hastings and started out for Detroit at about one o'clock. I tried to take a nap, my feet burning from the heater. An hour later we lurched to a wild stop on the shoulder. Mike had fallen asleep and Sam had grabbed the wheel. Sam volunteered to drive but we had to push the seat forward, since he is only five feet five.

Mike left us, cheerfully, at the Detroit airport about dawn and we slept for an hour and a half before flying on to Indianapolis for a concert at Clews Hall. Everything went beautifully and I began to think we'd broken the jinx.

The next day we flew to Downey Grove, Illinois. A reporter was supposed to meet us at the airport. This time I knew of the arrangements. She wasn't there.

The sponsor said, "Well, I explained to her that you didn't like to meet the press."

I couldn't believe it. For twenty years I'd had fine relations with newspapermen, radio and TV people. Now this. It seemed like a plot. I remember clapping my hand on top of my head.

He talked on. It was a Sunday and some religious group had gathered two hundred signatures on a petition to stop the concert. They claimed I was in "league with the Devil."

Whatever league I was in, the performance started on time. After it was over, a spokesman for about fourteen people said,

"How about us taking you out to dinner?" I was starved and immediately agreed. At the end of the meal the waitress dropped the check for all sixteen of us into my lap.

We flew on to Chicago for a suburban night-club appearance. A limo picked us up and I went to the motel near the club to find local press people who had been waiting for more than an hour. By this time I had a stock answer: "No one told me."

I had requested a small folding screen to be placed on the stage, and on arrival found they'd nailed it to the backing. A claw hammer solved that, but didn't solve the warm-up emcee, who I was told also played the accordion between shows at the club. Sam came back to the dressing room to say, "There's a guy out there telling jokes that couldn't live in a sewer." Some of the audience was already leaving. I went out earlier than anticipated.

At 1 A.M. we went on to Butler Airport, a private field in Chicago. The night club had chartered an aircraft to fly us to Saginaw, Michigan, where I had a 10 A.M. Town Hall performance. There was no plane. After five or six phone calls we learned that the limo driver had taken us to the wrong airport. The right one was two hours' driving distance.

I think it was about 3 A.M. when the aircraft finally landed at Butler and got us airborne for Saginaw; it was well after 4 A.M. when we arrived. The temperature was fifteen degrees below zero. There was no one to meet us, the sponsor having wisely given up and gone home to bed. We made it to the same position about five-thirty, with a wake-up call for eight.

Except for the fact that the stage crew was in a quarrelsome mood and wanted to strike, everything in Saginaw went fine.

That afternoon I bid good-bye to Sam in Detroit. For the remaining three days I'd be in professional hands—show-business people. I was scheduled for New Orleans, a convention of the National Association of TV Broadcasters. I was very excited about that appearance. I would share the honors with Bishop Fulton Sheen.

The Braniff plane took off for New Orleans, arriving over the Mississippi in a violent thunderstorm. After circling and bouncing for thirty minutes, we went over to Shreveport, where we circled and bounced some more, finally going on to Dallas. Five minutes after landing we were off again to New Orleans. It was a fruitless flight. Back at Dallas, we waited for another thirty minutes. Finally, at 11 P.M., we landed in New Orleans, one half-hour after the anticipated Bishop Sheen-Kreskin appearance was over. I later heard that the bishop was magnificent.

No one was at the airport to shepherd me to the hotel. Having averaged three hours' sleep a night, nerves shot, near exhaustion, I made it to the convention headquarters to learn that my lodging was supposedly across the street in another hotel. However, there'd been another slip-up. After two hours, it became apparent there was no room in town.

At 3 A.M. I called a convention executive to announce that I was headed for Newark; I'd had it. He came scurrying over and offered a company's hospitality room. Apologizing for the fact that someone had erred on reservations, he said, "Kres, you gotta be professional." I was trying.

We went to the hospitality room. It was wall-to-wall chaos with empty liquor bottles and full ashtrays. There was a small bedroom off on one side. We went in. It was filled with TV sets and spotlights, but there was a bed in it.

The executive said, "When you wake up, we'll get you a room." He left in haste.

I thought about taking a shower and went into the bathroom. The shower was filled with mattresses. There was another bedroom on the opposite side of the suite. That shower had assorted storage.

I'm not sure why I did it, but I decided to go for a walk. It was daybreak when I got back and turned in. About two o'clock the phone rang. It was Lou Reda in Easton. He said, "I've heard, I've heard. There's a vice-president who's been sitting out in the reception room all day, guarding it. He's been afraid to knock on your door. Go out and say hello."

I performed for the TV broadcasters later that afternoon and then flew to Chicago for a night-club date that night. I wasn't at all surprised when it was announced that O'Hare Field was iced up, and we'd have to hold over Milwaukee. We circled twenty or thirty times and then landed. I had twenty minutes to make the show.

Operating now in a complete mental fog, I decided to keep going, or else collapse, and took a flight to Newark about 2 A.M. Of course Newark was fogged in and we couldn't land at six as scheduled. Instead we went to La Guardia. At that airport I called my sister-in-law to say I would arrive by taxi. Otherwise, I was certain I'd get on a helicopter bound for Staten Island.

As I was making the call I watched a man and a woman stop outside the phone booth. The man picked up my bags and headed away. I dropped the phone and ran after him. Yelling for him to stop, he pointed at the woman and said, "I thought they were hers."

So ends the absolutely true account of *Concert Tour No. 1, 1973.* But it isn't always like that. Only sometimes.

Unless I'm on a college show, which can often lead to a lively, serious discussion of ESP with students after the curtain, I prefer the hotel room and TV or reading. I'm usually back in the room within an hour, having had late supper. If there's a good horror movie, especially anything Gothic, I try to sandwich it in between shows. I read a half-dozen books a week and also relax by playing chess or cards. Hearts is aggressive without building the tension of bridge. Pinochle is fun and I've got steady pinochle partners in twenty or thirty cities. In fact, I sometimes code forthcoming engagements by the names of my pinochle partners rather than by city names.

Aside from dining occasionally with close friends in one

place or another, it's basically the lonely life of any performer on a schedule of many one-night stands. At home, the few days of the month that I can call my own, I relax by playing the piano. I also enjoy camping and hiking but seldom have the time.

Yet I love the life and never really think about doing anything else. Unhappy when I'm not working, I constantly complain to Lou that I'm overbooked and never have the time to do the things I'd like to do. That, too, is typical of most performers. Those who know better ignore it.

Money has never been as important as breaking through some new area or application of ESP, of having a stubborn physical effect finally work. Then there are those goals that everyone has. Long ago, when playing to my Polish relatives at St. Michael's Hall in Bethlehem, I vowed I'd someday appear in Carnegie Hall. In early 1973 I did a one-man show in that hallowed theater.

The only people I was really looking for beyond the footlights were the Poles from Bethlehem and Allentown, friends and relatives from Caldwell, and the Catholic fathers from Seton Hall. About fifty of my kin arrived on West Fifty-seventh Street that Saturday night, a street they seldom visit. This may all sound like a corny page out of a vaudeville movie but I don't know any performer who doesn't have a lifelong dream of one special room in which to show his wares, to realize a youthful ambition.

Another milestone might have occurred. I could well be the only entertainer who has ever played "Chopsticks" on Carnegie's grand piano. It was a musical sacrilege I couldn't resist. Ignace Paderewski, another good Pole, might have turned over in his grave. I doubt it, though. Mr. Edison never completed his machine for spirit contact.

Autobiographies are usually written late in life but I consider what has gone into these pages as a midway account rather than an autobiography. Hopefully, I'll explore and experiment with ESP and suggestibility for a long time to come. There is so much to learn.

I think the human mind awaits many new and startling uses. Regretfully, we seldom call upon it to do more than it did yesterday, or a thousand years ago.

SELECT BIBLIOGRAPHY

with author's comments

Abbott, David P., *Behind the Scenes with the Mediums* (Chicago, The Open Court Publishing Company, 1907). *An interesting account of deceptions during the heyday of spiritualism.*

Barber, T. X., *Hypnosis—A Scientific Approach* (New York, Van Nostrand Reinhold, 1969). *In my opinion, probably the most important collection of findings in scientific research of hypnotic phenomena seen in this century.*

Baudouin, C., *Suggestion and Autosuggestion* (London, Allen & Unwin, 1920). *An early work well worth evaluating.*

Bennett, Colin, *Hypnotic Power* (London, Occult Book Society, n.d.). *A simple but strangely intriguing book by a lay therapist.*

Bernheim, H., *Suggestive Therapeutics* (Westport, Conn., Associated Booksellers, 1957. Originally published: 1886). *A pioneering classic written during the "golden age" of hypnotic phenomena.*

Bernstein, M., *The Search for Bridey Murphy* (Garden City, N.Y., Doubleday, 1956). *This single book triggered a wave of controversy through the Western world on the subject of reincarnation.*

Bjornstrom, F., *Hypnotism* (New York, Humbolt Publishing Company, 1887). *An alarmist account by a psychiatrist.*

Bolen, J. G., ed., *Psychics* (New York, Harper & Row, 1972). *The editor of* Psychic *magazine has included nine in-depth interviews, including one with the author of this book.*

Bramwell, J. M., *Hypnotism* (London, Grant Richards, 1903). *Author of the period of Bernheim.*

BIBLIOGRAPHY

Brandon, J., *Successful Hypnotism* (New York, Stravon Publishers, 1956). *A program book for the performer.*

Brennan, M., and Gill, M. M., *Hypnotherapy* (New York, International Universities Press, 1967). *A psychoanalytic perspective in "hypnotic" treatment.*

Brown, Slater, *The Heyday of Spiritualism* (New York, Hawthorn Books, 1970). *A spicy history difficult to put aside.*

Burton, Jean, *Heyday of a Wizard: Daniel Home the Medium* (London, Harrap, 1948). *A "biography" of a medium.*

Carrington, Hereward, *The Physical Phenomena of Spiritualism* (Boston, Small Maynard and Company, 1908). *A monumental work on fraudulent spiritualism.*

————, and Fodor, Nandor, *Haunted People* (New York: Dutton, 1951). *Both authors believed in the possibility of true poltergeists.*

Carter, M. E., *My Years with Edgar Cayce* (New York, Harper & Row, 1972). *A more recent personalized account of Edgar Cayce and his work, written by his secretary.*

Christopher, Milbourne, *ESP, Seers, and Psychics* (New York, Crowell, 1970). *We are treated, in part, with lengthy discussions of animal and side-show acts.*

————, *Houdini: The Untold Story* (New York, Crowell, 1969). *Newspaper-style report of Houdini's life.*

————, *Panorama of Magic* (New York, Dover, 1962). *A beautiful pictorial history of stage magic.*

Clareus, C., *An Illustrated History of the Horror Films* (New York, Putnam's, 1967). *Brilliant and scholarly; a study of the visual and auditory fascination of the mind through Gothic horror movies.*

Cocke, J. R., *Hypnotism* (Boston, Arena Publishing Company, 1894). *Typical popular book, reflecting professional interest of the period.*

Coué, Émile, *Self-Mastery through Conscious Autosuggestion* (London, Allen & Unwin, 1951). *Originally published in 1922. This is the author who made "autosuggestion" internationally popular.*

Doyle, Sir Arthur Conan, *The Complete Sherlock Holmes* (Garden City, N.Y., Doubleday, 1930). *What irony that Doyle would feud with Houdini over spiritualism!*

Drake, D., *Horror* (New York, Macmillan, 1966). *The author errs at times in his enthusiastic descriptions of the horror film.*

Duke, Mark, *Acupuncture* (New York, Pyramid House, 1972). *Only passing mention is made of suggestion.*

Ebon, Martin, ed., *Psychic Discoveries by the Russians* (New York, New American Library, 1971). *A collection of papers by or about Russian researchers. Worth reading.*

Elman, Dave, *Findings in Hypnosis* (Clifton, N.J. Published by author, 1964). *Radio's* Hobby Lobby *seemed to interest doctors in suggestive therapeutics.*

BIBLIOGRAPHY

Elworthy, T. F., *The Evil Eye* (London, Collier, 1958). *An excellent historical study of superstition.*

Erickson, M. H., Hershman, S., and Secter, I. I., *The Practical Applications of Medical and Dental Hypnosis* (New York, Julian Press, 1961). *Very weak in content; not worth the price.*

Esdaile, J., *Hypnosis in Medicine and Surgery* (New York, Julian Press, 1957. Originally published: 1850). *Historical curiosity.*

Estabrooks, G. H., ed., *Hypnosis: Current Problems* (New York, Harper & Row, 1962). *Better than his earlier book (below) because of the contributors.*

Estabrooks, G. H., *Hypnotism* (New York, Dutton, 1943). *Long considered the first American authoritative source, it is replete with distortions and unproven "facts."*

Ford, Arthur, in collaboration with Margueritte Harmon Brother, *Nothing So Strange* (New York, Harper's, 1958). *The "life" of the controversial medium, with the myth of breaking the Houdini code kept intact.*

Forel, A., *Hypnotism* (New York, Allied Publications, 1949). *A reprint of a classical work.*

Fredericks, Carlton, and Goodman, Herman, *Low Blood Sugar and You* (New York, Constellation International, 1969). *An interesting commentary on how low blood sugar may affect mental perception.*

Fuller, J. G., *The Interrupted Journey* (New York, Dial, 1966). *Therapeutic "hypnosis" (we are told) is used to reveal a UFO sighting and abduction aboard a spaceship.*

Gardner, Martin, *Fads and Fallacies in the Name of Science* (New York, Dover, 1957). *Includes a jaundiced view of ESP.*

Gibson, W. B., and Gibson, L. R., *The Complete Illustrated Book of the Psychic Sciences* (Garden City, N.Y., Doubleday, 1966). *An extensive and almost encyclopedic presentation.*

Hansel, C. E. M., *ESP: A Scientific Evaluation* (New York, Scribner's, 1966). *In the name of science, a remarkably biased debunking of all parapsychological research.*

Hargrave, C. P., *A History of Playing Cards* (New York, Dover, 1966). *Fascinating romance of playing cards.*

Hilgard, E. R., *Hypnotic Susceptibility* (New York, Harcourt, Brace & World, 1965). *Read it with skeptical glasses.*

Holzer, Hans, *Predictions: Fact or Fallacy?* (New York, Hawthorn, 1968). *By the famous ghost hunter. Holzer may be the outstanding science fiction writer in parapsychology.*

Hull, C. L., *Hypnosis and Suggestibility: An Experimental Approach* (New York, Appleton Century, 1933). *The "first" of experimental textbooks on "hypnosis." Dull reading.*

Hynek, J. Allen, *The UFO Experience: A Scientific Inquiry* (Chicago,

Regnery, 1972). *A brilliant search into UFO phenomena by a man who admits the role suggestibility might play.*

Janet, P., *Psychological Healing*, Vol. I (New York, Macmillan, 1925). *The author was influenced by Charcot and his theories of hysteria.*

Journal of the American Society for Psychical Research (New York). *This is an internationally respected, highly conservative quarterly which should be in the hands of all serious students.*

Kline, M. V., *Hypnodynamic Psychology* (New York, Julian Press, 1955). *The title alone should scare people away.*

Kroger, W. S., *Childbirth with Hypnosis* (Garden City, N.Y., Doubleday, 1961). *A book for the general reader in an area of diminishing popularity.*

Kuhn, L., and Russo, S., *Modern Hypnosis* (New York, Psychological Library Publishers, 1947). *Not as modern as it is historically interesting.*

LaCron, L. M., *Experimental Hypnosis* (New York, Macmillan, 1952). *Some interesting contributions and articles. The author's credentials should not strengthen the worth of this material.*

————, and Bordeaux, J., *Hypnotism Today* (New York, Grune & Stratton, 1947). *Much better than Estabrooks.*

Leitner, K., *Master Key to Hypnotism* (New York, Stavon Publishers, 1950). *The "master key" is deep breathing! Slightly incredible.*

Mackay, Charles, *Memoirs of Extraordinary Popular Delusions and the Madness of Crowds* (London, Routledge, 1892). *Fascinating accounts which give insight into mob psychology.*

Maltz, Maxwell, *Psycho-Cybernetics* (Hollywood, Calif., Wilshire Book Company, 1971). *Superficial techniques of using the imagination with autosuggestion, but worth studying.*

Marks, W. M., *The Story of Hypnotism* (New York, Prentice-Hall, 1947). *A fast-moving history; noteworthy for the author's commentaries on many movements.*

Marcuse, F. L., *Hypnosis: Fact and Fiction* (Baltimore: Penguin Books, 1959). *I found it difficult to distinguish fact from fiction.*

Marmer, M. J., *Hypnosis in Anesthesiology* (Springfield, Ill., C. C. Thomas, 1959). *One will suspect that the natural-childbirth schools may have more to offer than "hypnosis."*

Maskelyne, N., and Devant, D., *Our Magic* (Berkeley Heights, N.J., Fleming Books Company, 1946). *Originally published in 1911, one of the most important works on conjuring ever written has been read by few.*

McConnell, R. A., *ESP Curriculum Guide* (New York, Simon & Schuster, 1971). *A modest guide for high school or early university courses on the subject.*

McNally, R. T., and Floresce, R., *In Search of Dracula* (Greenwich,

Conn., New York Graphic Society, 1972). *Many of the fears, delusions and artifacts of occult power are encompassed in "Dracula." Excellent.*

Moll, A., *The Study of Hypnotism* (New York: Julian Press, 1958. Originally published: 1889). *A classic similar to the works of Bernheim and Bramwell.*

Montgomery, Ruth, *A Gift of Prophecy* (New York, Morrow, 1965). *Jeane Dixon's recountings. Enough said.*

Moss, A. A., *Hypnodontics: Hypnosis in Dentistry* (Brooklyn, N.Y., Dental Items of Interest Publishing Company, 1952). *Better left unread by the busy dentist.*

Murphy, Gardner, *Challenge of Psychical Research* (New York, Harper Colophon Books, 1961). *Gardner Murphy is one of a half-dozen true twentieth-century pioneers in the U.S.A.*

Parkyn, H. A., *Suggestive Therapeutics and Hypnotism* (Hollywood, Calif., Wilshire Book Company, 1958). *A typical mail-order course popular at the early part of this century.*

Pike, James A., with Diane Kennedy, *The Other Side* (Garden City, N.Y., Doubleday, 1968). *It all started with the Ford-Pike séance.*

Podmore, F., *From Mesmerism to Christian Science* (New Hyde Park, N.Y., University Books, 1963. Originally published: 1909). *A fascinating chronology of the movements to arise out of magnetism.*

Pollack, J. H., *Croiset The Clairvoyant* (New York, Bantam Books, 1965). *A remarkable book about a remarkable person.*

Prince, F. P., *Noted Witnesses for Psychic Occurrences* (New Hyde Park, N.Y., University Books, 1963). *A brilliant pioneer in occult research.*

Psychic magazine (San Francisco, The Bolen Company). *A bimonthly periodical with responsible editing (J. G. Bolen, ed.).*

Reiff, R., and Scheerer, M., *Memory and Hypnotic Age Regression* (New York, International Universities Press, 1959). *One should bear in mind that maturity tests in "regressed" subjects show no real regression.*

Reiter, P. J., *Antisocial or Criminal Acts and Hypnosis: A Case Study* (Springfield, Ill., C. C. Thomas, 1958). *An unsuccessful attempt to "prove hypnosis" was significant in the Denmark case.*

Rhine, Joseph B., *Extra-sensory Perception* (London, Faber & Faber, 1935). *The beginning of the controversy and of Rhine's great contributions.*

————, *New World of the Mind* (New York, Sloane, 1953). *Stuffy, repetitious, and dull reading.*

Rinn, J. F., *Sixty Years of Psychical Research* (New York, The Truth Seeks Company, 1950). *By a man who knew Houdini but whose memory was failing when he wrote his story.*

Robert-Houdin, Jean E., *Memoirs of Robert-Houdin* (Minneapolis, Carl W. Jones, 1944). *The nineteenth-century autobiography of the man often called the "the father of modern magic."*

Scarne, John, *Scarne's Complete Guide to Gambling* (New York, Simon & Schuster, 1961). *The gambling expert offers a cut to protect victims against card cheats, but it's not the protection one is led to believe.*

Sheen, Fulton J., *Peace of Soul* (Garden City, N.Y., Garden City Books, 1951). *By a man who must, in his love for God and mankind, have achieved what his book title implies.*

————, *Life Is Worth Living* (New York, McGraw-Hill, 1953). *Scripts of the legendary TV series which made the bishop a household word.*

Sidis, B., *The Psychology of Suggestion* (New York, Appleton, 1910). *Should be read by all serious students.*

Sinclair, Upton, *Mental Radio* (New York, Collier, 1971). *Written in 1930, the book has become a classic in telepathy and contains a meaningful commentary by Albert Einstein.*

Smith, Suzy, *Confessions of a Psychic* (New York, Macmillan, 1971). *A highly personalized biographical account by one of the most prolific popular writers in the field.*

Snyder, E. D., *Hypnotic Poetry* (Philadelphia, University of Pennsylvania, 1930). *Poetry which is supposed to create a hypnotic state! What?*

Spraggett, Allen, *The Unexplained* (New York, New American Library, 1967). *Spraggett condemns those who claim that Arthur Ford practiced fraud.*

St. Clair, David, *The Psychic World of California* (Garden City, N.Y., Doubleday, 1972). *Why, oh why, do there seem to be so many psychics in California?*

Stearn, Jess, *The Door to the Future* (Garden City, N.Y., Doubleday, 1963). *All the more interesting because Stearn originally set out to expose fraudulent cases of ESP but changed his mind.*

Steger, M., *Hypnoidal Therapy* (New York, Froben, 1951). *The use of a "state" preceding "hypnosis." I pass.*

Stoker, Bram, *Dracula* (New York, Pocket Books, Inc., 1947. Originally published: 1897). *Stoker's legendary character was skillfully created to strike fear in the minds of readers (and moviegoers). A masterpiece.*

Thurston, Howard, *My Life of Magic* (Philadelphia, Dorrance, 1929). *A ghosted autobiography of the great stage magician.*

Volgyesi, F. A., *Hypnosis of Man and Animals* (Hollywood, Wilshire Book Company, 1968). *Traditional Russian confusion of animal and human "hypnotic" response.*

Ward, D., ed., *Favorite Stories of Hypnotism* (New York, Dodd, Mead,

1965). *Commentaries by Dr. Milton V. Kline precede each mystery and horror story. The fiction is the best part of the book.*

Weitzenhoffer, A. M., *General Techniques of Hypnotism* (New York, Grune Stratton, 1957). *A detailed description of "hypnotic" induction techniques, including a large coverage of those used for stage "hypnosis."*

————, *Hypnotism: An Objective Study in Suggestibility* (New York, Wiley, 1953). *Weitzenhoffer's subjective study.*

Wells, W. R., "Experiments in Waking Hypnosis for Instructional Purposes," *J. Abnormal Social Psychology,* 1924, New York. *A tentative questioning of the necessity or even lack of a "hypnotic" trance.*

Wolberg, L. R., *Hypnoanalysis* (New York, Grune and Stratton, 1945). *There may be a contradiction in combining "hypnotic" suggestion with analytic techniques.*

Wydenbruck, N., *Doctor Mesmer* (London, John Westhouse, 1947). *An idyllic biography.*

Young, P. C., "Hypnotic Regression—Fact or Artifact?," *J. Abnormal Social Psychology,* 1940, New York. *An interesting weighing of both sides of the issue.*

Zilboorg, G., and Henry, G. W., *A History of Medical Psychology* (New York, Norton, 1941). *An extensive suggestion has played a role in this history.*